MW01289173

Top Secrets for Using LinkedIn to Promote Your Business or Yourself

by Gini Graham Scott, Ph.D.

Author of a Dozen Books on Work, Professional Development, and Promotion, including *Doing Your Own PR; Want It, See It, Get It!* and *Enjoy! 101 Little Ways to Add Fun to Your Work Everyday*

iUniverse, Inc.
New York   Bloomington

Copyright © 2010 by Gini Graham Scott

All rights reserved. No part of this book may be used or reproduced by any means,
graphic, electronic, or mechanical, including photocopying, recording, taping or by any
information storage retrieval system without the written permission of the publisher
except in the case of brief quotations embodied in critical articles and reviews.

iUniverse books may be ordered through booksellers or by contacting:

iUniverse
1663 Liberty Drive
Bloomington, IN 47403
www.iuniverse.com
1-800-Authors (1-800-288-4677)

Because of the dynamic nature of the Internet, any Web addresses or links contained in this book
may have changed since publication and may no longer be valid. The views expressed in this work
are solely those of the author and do not necessarily reflect the views of the publisher, and the
publisher hereby disclaims any responsibility for them.

ISBN: 978-1-4502-1898-6 (sc)

Printed in the United States of America

iUniverse rev. date: 05/10/2010

Table of Contents

Introduction

This book is designed to help you use LinkedIn to promote your business or yourself -- or if you are already on LinkedIn to help you expand your effectiveness. Even though there are other popular social networking sites, such as Twitter and Facebook, LinkedIn is the premier business-oriented service for connecting people who want to do business together. It currently has over 60 million members in over 150 industries and over 200 countries and territories around the world. Executives from all of the Fortune 500 companies are LinkedIn members.

To illustrate the tips and techniques I'm discussing, I have included examples from my own LinkedIn account and about two dozens screenshots as a guide. Use these to help you create your own powerful presence on the Internet and let your contacts -- and often their contacts -- know what you are doing and how you can help them. Ideally, have your computer open to your LinkedIn account to follow along as you read this.

I developed this book as a guide to accompany a series of workshops and seminars I have been doing on using the social media to promote oneself and expand one's business. I developed the material for these workshops and seminars and this guide as a result of using LinkedIn and the other social media to promote my own books, films, and TV projects over the last three years.

In the process, I participated in several workshops led by social media experts and worked with a social media consultant, who advised me and several employees who were working for me. I received several writing assignments for books and films as a result of clients I met through LinkedIn, have provided people in my network with advice and received advice from them, and have attended a number of events organized by people in my network.

Please note that I am writing this as an individual business owner with a LinkedIn account. I am not a representative of and have no other affiliation with LinkedIn.

Part 1: The Basics Of Getting Started The Right Way

Chapter 1: Creating a Powerful Linked In Profile

A first step to using LinkedIn is to create a complete and compelling profile.

A reason for this is that having a presence on LinkedIn will help get your name, Website, and profile to the top of the search engines. So you want your profile to be a strong selling point for your company, product, or service when people first come to your site. Even if you already have a strong Web presence, build your LinkedIn profile. Moreover, the more information and key words you put in your LinkedIn profile, the more that will help you with search engine optimization (SEO).

For example, my own LinkedIn site, which I'm using to illustrate how to use LinkedIn, comes up 5th, but that's because I already have a very active blog site, Wikipedia entry, and books on Amazon. If I didn't, my LinkedIn profile would be in 2nd or 3rd position.

Another reason to have a completed profile is that when someone goes to your profile to learn who you are, whether they're a potential client or prospective employer, you want to put your best foot forward. Your LinkedIn profile is like having a resume or posting your credentials online.

For example, at workshops I have repeatedly heard that researchers have found that 85% of employers before extending an offer will review a candidate's LinkedIn profile in doing a background check. So you want to make sure you have as much information in your profile as possible.

Creating Your Headline

Your name and your headline are the first thing that people see when they go to your LinkedIn profile. First they see your name and then they see a second line which is your headline. Don't use the headline to list your title and the name of your company, which are already listed under "Current." There is no reason to waste space with a headline that tells someone what they will find when they look down and see the same information at your current position.

Also, use your headline to convey something about your business, since LinkedIn is a business networking site. Thus, if you want to promote what you did this past weekend or let people know that you like to ski or surf, use Facebook or another site that features fun activities. The purpose of LinkedIn is to promote business networking to build business relationships.

Accordingly, in writing your headline, you might write something like: "Entrepreneur, Social Media Expert, and Business-to-Business Marketing Specialist." Use three or four descriptive terms to create an eye-catching headline, so when people see your profile, they will see what you specialize in right away. Think of it this way: in business you typically have about 5-10 seconds to catch people's attention. So use your headline to do just that.

To enter your display name and your headline, go to the Edit My Profile tab, and fill in the Basic Information boxes with this information.

Creating Your Summary

As part of completing your profile, complete your summary, too. Consider this summary a snapshot to draw people to want to do business with you.

For example, in your summary, you might highlight you the professional but include a little bit about you the person. You can be unique in your summary, as well as provide details to feature the main things you do in one business or a number of businesses. Thus, you might note some of the specific services that your company provides or promote your multiple businesses. Avoid having an incomplete summary, so fill it up with as much information as possible.

It's best to update your summary once a month with fresh content, just as it's preferable to keep your Website current. Keeping your summary updated regularly will not only provide information for clients, but help with your SEO, so you optimize your opportunities for search engines to find you. The process is the same as adding new content to improve the SEO for your Website. If you don't have time to keep your profile updated yourself, find a local or virtual assistant to post new information, such as new products, services, or news about your company or yourself.

In short, think of your summary as a way to engage people to want to do business with you. Thus, don't only talk about yourself, but talk about how you can help people, since people want to know how you might assist them in making their own business grow. Then, if they think you can help them, they will want to know more about you. So always try to find ways to give value and help people.

Describing Your Specialties

The Specialties section is where to put the main types of products and services you provide. Use as many common keywords as possible, since this will not only help prospective customers and clients see what you offer, but it will help the search engines find you. When they do, you will come up higher in the rankings when prospects put in these words in a search.

If you have specialties in different fields, include them all. For example, one woman at a workshop had one business offering health services and a place that could be used for meetings. Plus she assisted with party planning and special events. In listing her specialties, she should include a number of terms related to health and to her party and event planning business. In another case, a man specialized in accounting and taxes, but also was proficient in Excel and database management. So he should put all of that in his list of specialties.

Describing Your Work Experience

Ideally, include your past five years of work experience in your LinkedIn profile, and some people even go back 10 years. The reason for including this detail about your past work is that when people search for you, they may look for you by the company where you worked. So suppose they know you from when you worked at XYZ Company, though now you're with the ABC Company. If you don't have the XYZ Company in your profile, when they do a search by your name, they may find multiple people with the same name as you. So they won't be able to tell whether someone with your name is you or not unless you have the XYZ Company in your LinkedIn profile.

Thus, go back at least five years, and if you're looking for work, it's even more important to have as much work experience in your LinkedIn profile as possible. Consider LinkedIn like having a second resume.

Listing Your Websites

LinkedIn also helps to drive traffic to up to three of your Websites. It has generic fields for Websites, which are "My Company," "My Blog," and "My Personal Website." While you can use these three, you can readily adapt them to list the most important Websites for you, if you go to "edit my profile" and choose "Other." But if you have a blog, keep that.

Since LinkedIn allows you to have three Websites on your profile, take advantage of that option, even if you only have one site for your business. In that case, use the other sites to refer to the most important organizations you belong to. For example, say you belong to a rotary chapter or a Business Network International (BNI) chapter. Put that organization in as one of your Websites. That way, even if someone isn't interested in your business, they may be looking for other resources, and this listing will help them find that. This way you are giving them value, which can help them think well of you and might lead to their business or to a referral to their contacts in the future.

Including Your Interests

Just below Websites, there is a section for including your interests. Include anything that is relevant here, and again, the words you use can be picked up by the search engines to help people in finding you.

Listing Your Groups and Associations

Here's where to include the groups and associations you belong to. List the ones that are most relevant to your business, and include the most important ones first. I've included an example of how I filled this out in the previous screenshot.

Listing Your Honors and Awards

Now if you have any relevant awards include those, again the most relevant and most important first. For example, I included an award I won about five years ago for obtaining a client who used my services connecting a client from Hong Kong to film producers and agents in the U.S. at an export event sponsored by the U.S. Department of Commerce's Export Division. But I left out awards I got for books over 15 years ago.

Using the Network Updates and Status Bar

The Status Bar is located on the LinkedIn Home Page, under Network Updates. I have found that this Status Bar is frequently underused, but it is important because this is how people in your network can track what you're doing on a regular basis. The larger your network, the more people will see your status update. In turn, you can use the Status Updates to track what others are doing.

The Status Bar is also especially useful, since many people are very busy and usually don't have the time to follow up with all the people they know on a daily basis. But if you read your contacts' Status Bar updates and click on "Show more" for additional information, you can keep up with them. Moreover, seeing these updates may lead you to recognize that this is an ideal time to contact someone to seek their business or get a lead from them because of what they are doing now. The update is a reminder to help you stay in touch at a good time for making contact.

Adding Network Updates

You can regularly let people in your immediate network know what you are doing by adding a short update in the box next to your name or picture box. Generally, the initial description is short -- up to 140 characters, though you can add additional details, which will show up as "Show More." After you enter the update in the box next to your picture and click "Share" it will appear under your box and be sent to people you are directly connected to in your network. Also, if you have a Twitter account and check the box next to the Twitter logo, your update will automatically go to your Twitter followers, too.

If you also are on other social media sites, such as Twitter, Facebook, and Plaxo, you can update all of these sites at the same time through a site called www.ping.fm. Through Ping, you can include all of the social networking sites you belong to in a single platform and update them all with a click of a button. You can easily sign up if you click the Signup button and then provide your email address and password.

Once you have your account, you simply list all of the social media sites you are a member of, type in your message of up to 140 words, and send it. Just click on "Add Social Networks" to see a complete list of the major social media you can participate in, and once you have an account with that social media site, you can send your message to that site as well as to LinkedIn through Ping. For example, I currently belong to Twitter, Facebook, Plaxo Pulse, and Yahoo Profiles in addition to Linked in. They are all listed as my default settings, so whatever message I enter will go to all of these.

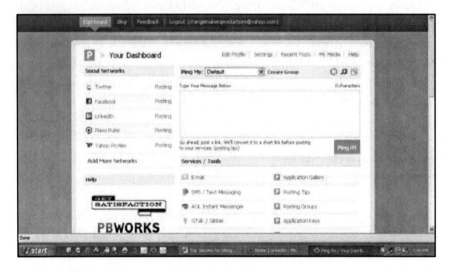

Ways to Use the Status Bar

Use the Status Bar to get more free promotion for you. You can use it to let people know what you are doing, announce new products and services, and refer people to interesting articles, Websites, and news, which adds value and helps people pay more attention to you.

Some people update their Status Bar frequently, even 3 or 4 times a day, though 1 to 2 times a day is more common. A good rule of thumb is to spend about 1/2 to 1 hours on LinkedIn in the morning and 1/2 to 1 hours in the evening. Or if you are more limited for time, you can spend only 15 minutes in the morning to note what you're looking forward that day and 15 minutes in the evening to indicate what you accomplished or found especially interesting.

Also, it helps to build relationships if you start replying to some of these status updates from others. You can reply privately or add a comment. Again keep the focus on how you can help the other person, rather than just saying what you have accomplished.

Using a Photo

Your photo helps to personalize you and your company. But it should be a business-like photo, such as a head shot or a head and shoulders shot. Avoid humorous photos or cartoons, because this is a professional networking site, and you're seeking to attract new business or are seeking a job. So you want to put your best foot forward in a professional photo.

If you don't have a recent picture of yourself, it's fine to use an older one for the time being. But it's preferable to post a recent one. You can get one at a local portrait shop, or to get a photo inexpensively, you might have a friend come over and take a photo of you.

Most people are now using digital cameras; otherwise use print film and have the photo processor put it on a CD as well as give you negatives and prints. This way, you can easily select the file to use for your photo and don't have to scan the print into a file yourself. Whatever type of camera you use, your photo should be saved in one of the popular photo formats, such as a small JPG, GIF, or PNG file, which can be uploaded at most online networking sites, as well as LinkedIn. Commonly, most photos on the Web are in a 72 dpi format, though generally you can upload any photo up to 200 or 300 dpi, as long as the file is under a specified file size limit.

To add your photo in LinkedIn, just go to "Edit My Profile" and upload your photo, as long as it's no larger than 4MB, in the "Upload a Photo" box. You can also specify whether you want your photo to be shown to your direct connections, your network which includes your 2nd and 3rd level and group connections, or to everyone who views your profile. Generally, to promote your company and yourself, make your photo visible to everyone.

Using Contact Settings

Your Contact Settings is where you indicate how people should get in touch with you. It's best to give people as many ways as possible to reach you. If you use Twitter or Facebook for business purposes, like I do, you can include your Twitter and Facebook usernames in your Contact Settings. You might also add your email and phone number, if these are ones you give out to the general public. Otherwise, LinkedIn advises that you should not include your contact information to avoid unwanted contacts, since it will be visible to everyone.

Also, let people know what type of messages you will accept, such as whether you will only accept Introductions or both Introductions and InMail. Note what type of requests you would like to receive under "Opportunity Preferences," such as whether you are interested in Career opportunities, Consulting offers, New ventures, Job inquiries, Expertise requests, Business deals, Personal reference requests, or Requests to reconnect. You can add advice on how you prefer to be contacted, too.

It's best to provide a variety of reasons for connecting with you to make it easier for people to contact you.

Chapter 2: Company Profiles and Connections

Besides creating your individual profile, you can create a company page with a profile as an owner or employee. If you are in more than one company, you can create a profile for each one. You can also learn more about the companies you are already connected to through your individual connections in each one. I'll discuss how to find companies in Chapter 7 on Using Search to Find Contacts and Information.

Adding a Company Profile

To add a company profile, go to the "More" tab and click on "Companies".

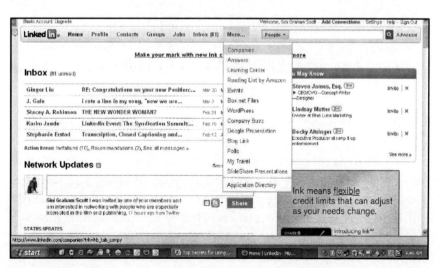

Then, click on "Add a Company." If you have already created a company profile, you'll see it there, but can add another.

To add a company, enter the company name and your email there.

However, you cannot use a personal email -- it has to be an email using the company's domain, or you will get a message that you can't use this. The one exception is if you use the same personal email for your company in opening your account.

Once you enter an email successfully, you have to check your inbox and confirm the email.

Adding Information to Your Company Profile

Once you confirm your email, you can add additional information about this company, though you will still use your primary email for your LinkedIn account. The company name and email will already be there, as in the example below, where I have created an additional company profile for the Film and TV Connection with its own email. After you create the listing, add the Website URL, description, type of industry, country, postal code, and your position in the company.

If you have a company logo, you can add that, too.

If you have more than one location for your company, such as branches in different cities, you can add additional locations.

You can also add the company financials or a company blog.

If you go to the company's profile, you will see how complete it is, along with a suggestion to help promote your company and complete your profile -- in this case by adding specialties. Meanwhile, LinkedIn will search for other employees who already are LinkedIn members to add to this page. Once you have fully completed your profile, you will see it listed, along with your name as a current employee.

Then, everyone can see your company on your profile, along with any other companies you have listed. Should you leave a company, you can always remove it.

Connecting with Other Companies

Just as you can connect with other people by name, so you can discover the companies where you already have connections. To do so, go to "More" and then "Companies", as noted above. Then, below your company profile, which will list the latest company profile you added first, you will see the companies in your network. Your own companies will be listed first, followed by the companies in which you have 1st level connections. Click "See more" to see a complete listing of all the companies where you have connections.

You will then see all the companies where you have 1st and 2nd degree connections, including how many people are employees, if you have more than a single connection. You will also see where each company's headquarters is located and the size of each company. For example, I have connections in over 8000 companies.

When you click on that company name, you will see all of your 1st and 2nd level connections in that company.

Finding and Becoming a Service Provider

You can find service providers or become listed as one, if you go to the "Service Providers" link from the "Companies" tab.

You'll then see an explanation about how the Service Provider Recommendations works, based on service providers getting recommendations by their clients. This listing features the services others have recommended and the number of recommendations each service provider has received. To get recommended yourself, ask your clients to recommend you.

Finding Recommended Providers

While the most recent recommendations are worldwide listings by default, you can limit them by location, including the top locations in San Francisco, New York, Los Angeles, and Washington, D.C. Or put in your own zip code.

Once you target the location, the recent recommendations in that area will be listed.

You can further zero in on the recent recommendations made by your 1st and 2nd degree contacts, such as these from my connections.

To see who you have recommended, click on "You."

Besides using these recommendations to select people for needed services, you can use recommendations as an entry to get connected. For example, you might send an inMail or get an introduction to that person from one of your own connections by saying you were impressed by their many recommendations, since sincere flattery often works well, and you hoped to talk with them further. Then, the door open, you can invite them to join your network or to send you an invite to get connected, as previously discussed.

You can also zero in on recommendations by category, using the listings in the Categories box on the right. These categories include Art, Creative and Media; Consulting; Employment Services; Financial and Legal Services; Health and Medical; Home and Garden; and Other Professional Services.

Then select a particular category. For example, after I selected Writers and Editors in the San Francisco Bay area, I found over 500 writers and editors recommended by all LinkedIn Users. But if I limited the recommendations to my 1st degree network, I found only 7, which included 3 for me, since I am also a writer in this area. There were 200 listings if I looked at 2nd degree recommendations.

Normally, you may prefer to look to your 1st degree connections for recommendation, since you know these people personally or are more closely connected. But you can broaden your search for service providers, if you don't find enough recommended providers locally.

Recommending Other Service Providers

You can recommend other providers, which is a good way to get them to recommend you. You can put in the names of people you want to recommend and their emails.

Or you can select from the list of people you are already connected to.

If you select from your own connections, LinkedIn will put in their name and email for you. Once you select who you want to recommend, click "Finished," you will get the recommendations menu to indicate the basis for your recommendation, as will be discussed in Chapter 3 on Using Recommendations. If the person has been a service provider, you would indicate that.

To request a recommendation from someone, go to "Request a Recommendation", also discussed in Chapter 3.

Chapter 3: Using Recommendations

Recommendations help to increase your credibility and help people feel good about doing business with you. Many people don't use recommendations as much as they should, though you can get them quite easily. Whenever you have satisfied clients or have done business with people successfully, why not ask them for recommendation?

Viewing Recommendations

The total number of recommendations you have received, except for hidden recommendations, show up on your public profile, indicated by the hands with the thumbs up. For example, on my LinkedIn profile, I have 11 recommendations, mainly as a result of asking people I know to give me one or giving a recommendation and getting one in return.

When you go to your full profile, by clicking "View Full Profile," you can see all of the people recommending you. If you have gotten these recommendations when working for different companies or for different businesses you own, you will see the names and number of people recommending you for each company listed separately. For example, there are 13 people listing me total, but 10 as the owner and CEO of Changemakers Productions, 2 as the owner and

CEO of Changemakers, and 1 as the owner and CEO of Creative Communications and Research.

Then, if you scroll down further, you will see each person's name and recommendation listed. If you have been recommended by people when you were identified with different companies, the recommendations are listed by the company with the most recommendations first.

If people click the names of people recommending you, they will go to the profile of the person making the recommendation to learn about that person. In turn, when you give someone a recommendation, this is a way to get recognition for yourself, too, since people can go to your profile.

Getting and Giving Recommendations

To get or give recommendations, go to your Profile and click on "Recommendations."

Then, that will take you to a page where you can manage your "Received Recommendations," see your "Sent Recommendations," or "Request Recommendations" from someone else. For example, if you go to "Received Recommendations," you will see the number of recommendations you have for each listed position.

You can send a request to someone to be endorsed for something by clicking "Ask to be endorsed." And if you scroll down on that page, you'll see where you can recommend others.

Once you click "Ask to be endorsed," that will take you to a screen where you can put in the company name and position for which you want to be recommended. You can send your request to up to 200 people at the same time.

If you want to ask people you are already connected to on LinkedIn, click the "In" box. Then you'll get a list of all of these people you can ask to recommend you. If you click the person's name, it will show up in the box to the right. To remove someone, click that person's name again.

If you already have a large list of people, you can limit your requests to people in a certain location or industry. Open up the "By Location" or "By Industry" menus to select the area or industry you want. Then, LinkedIn will narrow down the list of people according to the people in the industry or area you designated.

When you send your request for a recommendation, you can use the message that LinkedIn already has written: "I'm sending this to you to ask....Thanks in advance for helping me out" followed by your name. Or you can add in a personalized message, such as "I really enjoyed meeting you at the networking event," as in the example below, or only use your personal message and delete LinkedIn's message entirely.

If you are sending message to a number of people at the same time, it will go out as an individual message to everyone. But make sure your personalized message applies to everyone, or send messages individually or to separate groups of people with a personalized message that fits everyone in the group.

The person you ask for an endorsement will get your message in their inbox.

If that person clicks on the "Endorse *********" button, he or she will be taken to his or her own LinkedIn account.

Conversely, if you receive a request from someone and click on the "Endorse *****" button, you will be taken to your own account where you can write a recommendation.

Once you (or the person you have asked to endorse you) clicks on "Write Recommendation," you or that person will then be asked in what capacity you know whoever has asked for the endorsement -- as a Colleague, who you worked with in the same company; as a Service Provider, who provided a service to you; or as a Business Partner, who you worked with in some way, other than as a client or colleague.

You (or the person endorsing you) will then be asked to clarify how you worked together, including the position you held at the time of the endorsement and the position of the person you are endorsing. Then you (or the person endorsing you) can write whatever you want.

After the person endorsing you sends you their recommendation, it will show up in your LinkedIn inbox, so you can review it and decide if you want to accept that recommendation or not. Conversely, if you send a recommendation to someone, he or she can treat your recommendation in the same way.

When you see the other person's recommendation, you can either show it or hide it, which you may want to do if someone sends you a recommendation for your work in two different capacities. It might look strange to show both recommendations.

Or if you don't like a recommendation or see errors in it, you can ask the person to send a modified and corrected replacement. As a LinkedIn message explains, you are asking the person to revise their recommendation, followed by the original copy, after which you can write in your suggested revision. For example, if the person has made a mistake in spelling you can correct that, or if you want the person to add more information, such as in the example below, indicate. Then, send your request to the person, who can send back their revised recommendation for you to approve. Once you get the revision back, you can show or hide it, as previously described.

Normally, it's best to accept a recommendation, since the person has done you a favor, and you don't want to offend someone by turning down their recommendation down. However, it is embarrassing for both of you to have a recommendation with spelling or grammatical errors. If you aren't sure if there is a misspelling, you can run spell check on your recommendations. Though you can tell someone what you would like the recommendation to read, it's generally best not to do so to avoid offending the person, unless you catch spelling or grammatical errors -- or you are close to each other, so the person won't be offended by your suggested changes.

Once you accept the recommendation, you will be invited to return the favor by endorsing the person who just recommended you. Then, your recommendation will be sent to that person for his or her approval, and he or she can choose to ask for any revisions or show or hide it.

Once you accepted a new recommendation, it will show up on your recommendations page unless you hide it.

If at any time you don't want to show a particular recommendation, you can hit "Edit" and unselect "Show," which will hide that recommendation.

In the event you send a recommendation request and haven't heard back for awhile, LinkedIn helps you manage this by including a list of pending recommendations under your list of recommendations. This list indicates when you originally sent your request, and if you want, you can click "Resend" to send another request to that person.

Some Ways to Get Recommendations by Giving or Asking for Them

A good way to get recommendations is to give them first, since the people you recommend will be invited to recommend you. One way to initiate these recommendations is to search for people in your network who you are close to or have done business with successfully, if you don't already have a recommendation from them. If you have already recommended a person, this will show up next to the name of that person.

If you haven't already recommended them, you can click "Recommend this person." It's good to do so without expecting a recommendation back, since people will generally appreciate this gesture, because it seems more altruistic and giving, than if you email them in advance to make giving them a recommendation a quid pro quo for them recommending you. But commonly, without your having to ask, you will get a recommendation, since the person you have recommended will send a recommendation back in the same spirit of reciprocity. If they don't, you can later request a recommendation from them.

You can also ask for a recommendation directly. To do so, go to your Profile, and click on "Recommendations" and then on "Request Recommendations." Select the position you want a recommendation for and decide who you'll ask for the recommendation. It's a process you can repeat again and again

If you want to see the recommendations you have sent, they are categorized by colleagues, service providers, business partners, and students, so you can see how many people you have recommended in each category. If you click on one of these categories, you will see only your recommendations for that.

Being Selective About Your Recommendations

Generally, it is beneficial to have a lot of recommendations, since these show that a number of people feel you have done a good job working for them or that they value your business and your qualifications, or both. There are some people who have 40, 50, or even more recommendations.

However, be sure any recommendations you show are valued recommendations, and you aren't just accumulating numbers. Also, don't include recommendations from people you don't trust or if you feel they have squandered their value in giving a recommendation, because they have recommended so many people. For example, a good reason not to include someone is if you think he or she is a high profile marketing person who is just giving and collecting recommendations, or if you think this person is a flake or has no ethics.

If you don't want someone's recommendation to show up on your profile, you don't have to put the recommendation there. If they later send you a message back asking "Why didn't you put my recommendation up, you can diplomatically give them a reason to avoid hurting their feelings or sparking a confrontation, such as saying that you have enough recommendations now or you don't want to put their recommendation on your profile at this time, because you want to highlight recommendations from people in a certain field.

While you can't delete a recommendation, you can hide it. You just have to uncheck "Show," and while you can see the recommendation, those who come to visit your site won't.

Chapter 4: The Importance of Groups

A great way to connect with others who have similar interests and promote yourself to a targeted market is through groups. They are a great marketing tool to reach out to people in a targeted market, since you can find a group on just about anything, whether you're looking for accountants, doctors, lawyers, whatever. LinkedIn allows you to join up to 50 groups, and you can enter and leave groups as often as you like.

Searching for Groups

To search for groups, go to the "Status Bar" along the top of the LinkedIn screen, where there is a category for "Groups". If you are already a member of any groups, these will show up in your "My Groups" page, along with discussions and comments from the people you are following.

Then, go to the "Groups Directory" to find groups you want to join.

When you first go to the directory, it will open up the "Featured Groups" as shown below. These will generally be groups that have advertised or have a high level of traffic, which includes the White House and the UCLA Anderson Alumni Network.

Finding Different Types of Groups

You can find groups in particular categories if you click on the down arrow under "All categories":

When you click a particular category, it will take you to a Search Results page that lists all of the groups and the number of groups in that category. The groups are listed by the number of members, with the groups with the most members first.

To help you decide which groups to join, look at both the description of the group and its size. This way you can select the most appropriate groups and those with the largest number of members.

Many groups are moderated by whoever started them and any assistants. In this case, the moderator will review your request to join the group or ask you why you want to join a particular group. As long as you give a reasonable answer related to the purpose of the group or your profile shows this, you will probably be approved to join.

Finding Groups in a Location

You can also find groups in a particular area. While I'm using groups in Los Angeles as an example, you can apply these techniques in any area. If you are in a small suburb of a metropolitan area, look for groups in the larger area. To most rapidly expand your contacts in your area, it's a good idea to join the top groups there, based on their size.

Also, you can join groups in an area that you want to reach out to, either by email or by making a personal contact with group members later. For example, if I'm interested in producing a film in Las Vegas, I might look for groups to join in that area to develop some contacts I can later meet when I arrive in the area.

Say you want to search for groups in the Los Angeles area. Put Los Angeles in the "Keywords" box and hit "Search," which will then show the largest groups in L.A.

For example, the top business groups in the L.A. area includes these. The first three are shown in the example above.

- Women 2 Women Business, which targets high profile women executives
- Orange County Executives (included in the L.A. area based on the U.S. Census), whichhas a separate Website for interacting with group members
- Sales and Marketing Professionals Promoting High Tech and Technology
- Southern California Venture Capital Community
- LinkedWorking Los Angeles,
- ThinkLA,

- Business Success Network

- Southern California Dealmakers Network

In some cases, a group may have its own Website platform to communicate with group members, rather than using LinkedIn, so they will send you a link to get to that platform. Then, you have to go to there to join their group. If you want to interact with the group members using that platform, that's fine. But it can be inconvenient when you are a member of multiple groups to have to go to another platform on a separate Website, so you may not want to join the group for that reason.

Finding Groups in an Industry

You can also find groups in a particular industry. Say you are involved in the entertainment or film industry. To find groups in that industry, just put in the words "film" or "entertainment" in the keywords box. You'll get some of the same listings as in an area search, since much of the film and entertainment industry is in L.A., though you'll find some differences. Thus, it's a good idea to put in a number of related keywords to identify all the groups you want to target.

Finding Networking Groups

If you are interested in networking generally, a good site to join is Top Linked, which is an open networker group. Another is LION, which stands for Linked In Open Network. These are people who will connect with anyone interested in networking, which can help you in building a large network.

Though you might not have a reason to do business with these people now, you may want to do so in the future. Another reason for joining a networking group is that the people in your network might have a connection with other people who could use your products or services. So it's advantageous to build a large network.

If you know the name of a group, you can search for it individually, such as if someone has recommended that you join the Sales and Marketing Professionals or Think L.A. Just put the name you are looking for in the keyword box.

The Power of Joining Groups

To promote your business, join as many groups as possible, though you can only have one profile yourself. But if you have a partner or assistant, they could create another profile and work in tandem with you. For example, if you have a health store and are seeking to produce independent films, you might have your co-owner or manager have a profile for the health store, while you create a profile for yourself in the film industry.

When you set up one profile for yourself and another for a close associate, it can make sense to keep your activities and contacts through LinkedIn separate. When you do so, you and your associate should sign up under different company names and have a different name and email for each company, so you clearly have two separate identities.

Once you are a group member, you can join subgroups within a group, which can be a good idea when you are part of a very large group which encompasses people with different interests.

There are several things you can do as a group participant. One of the most important activities is to participate in discussions featured on the "Discussions" tab, which is a good way to let your connections know what your company is doing.

For example, one man uses discussions regularly and increases his presence with a weekly marketing blog every Sunday night, which he posts on every group he belongs to. He has found it especially valuable to post regularly, because people get accustomed to reading his discussions every Monday morning to see the new information he has provided. Since he has accumulated a large audience that follows him regularly, he continues to keep them engaged with these frequent posts. After he posts his blog, he typically gets over 50 responses in his LinkedIn inbox, and he gets comments from regular readers to let him know that they appreciate what he is doing. As an example, one morning several people took the time to comment on how thankful they were for the information he provided. If he stopped his regular postings, he might begin to lose his regular following.

What to Discuss

Discussions are a great way to build an audience for the different things you are doing in your business. For example, if you have an upcoming event or special promotion, create a discussion about this.

When you post these discussions in numerous groups, your audience builds up rapidly. For example, some groups may have over 500 people, others over 1000 or 5000 or more. Thus, when you post in multiple groups, you can quickly get your message out to many thousands of people in the short time it takes to post in each group -- say an hour to post in 30 groups reaching 30,000 people.

One marketing executive got over two dozen people to attend an event he was having in Las Vegas by joining several dozen groups in Nevada and promoting his LinkedIn event in those groups.

Using Your Signature in Your Postings

Whenever you post, though many people don't do this, put your signature with your contact information in your post, so people have an immediate way to contact you; they don't have to connect with you only through LinkedIn first.

Adapting Your Postings to the Group

Adapt your postings to what is appropriate in a particular group. While some group moderators allow anyone to join and post anything, many others are quite selective about the content they allow group members to post.

Often general discussions about a topic or announcing a free event are fine. But if you have an event, product, or service that involves a charge, the moderator will not permit that, or may do so on a case by case basis, depending on whether he or she feels you are offering a valuable activity, product, or service which is suitable for group members. Sometimes moderators will be more receptive if some or all of the funds are going to a charitable cause or if there is a special discount for group members. On the other hand, if someone posts something involving money, such as saying: "I have a product on a special this week" or "Buy 10 cases for xyz amount of dollars and save xxx percent," some group moderators will delete that post.

Given these different policies in groups, it's a good idea to notice what is acceptable in a group by seeing what others are posting. Or if you're not sure whether a moderator will accept or delete your post, you can take a chance and see what happens. If the moderator deletes it, and possibly sends you a note to explain why, you know for next time not to post something like that again. And once warned, be careful you don't do so, since a moderator will commonly regard the first inappropriate post as a learning experience, so you know what to not do next time. But if you post something inappropriate a second or third time that could be grounds for expulsion from the group, and afterwards, you often won't be able to rejoin.

Another thing to avoid is posting discussions that are not relevant to a group. For instance, if you are participating in a film group, keep your discussion related to films. Then, even if the posting involves an admission fee or cost for a product or service, you might still be able to post such information. By contrast, if you are promoting something not film related, even if it might be of interest to those in the film industry, you might not be able to post this, such as if you want to sell life insurance to producers.

Pacing Your Postings

How often should you post in a discussion? Generally, about one to three times a week is fine. Sometimes in very active groups, once a day might work well. Plus post your responses to others' new posts or their responses to you. For example, at a workshop, a sales coach described how he posted a discussion every other day, and he got a number of referrals from people who read his postings which featured tips on how to be successful in sales.

To decide how often to post, get a sense of how often others are posting in a group. Though many posters do so only occasionally or rarely, don't use them for pacing your own postings. Rather look for the frequency of the regular posters, aside from the group moderator, who will normally post much more frequently than anyone else in the group. Then, use the postings of these regulars as a guide. This way, if you follow the norms of the group's regulars, you will avoid wearing out your welcome in the group, since doing too much promotional posting could be grounds for removal from the group.

Also, check for responses to your discussions. Whenever someone else comments on your discussion, you'll get a message from LinkedIn in your email saying that someone has commented on your post.

Keep in mind that these discussions generally work best as a two way street. So if you want people to comment on the discussions you start, comment on their discussions, too.

Keeping Track of New Discussions and Posts

One way to track new discussions is to check the emails that come to your inbox from the members of your groups. Another way is to go to your homepage and go to "Group Updates." Then, you'll see what's going on in the groups you belong to, as in the screen shot below.

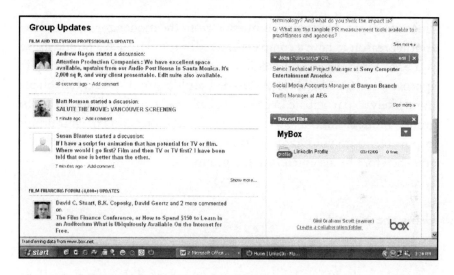

If you want to get updates more or less frequently, you can change the settings for how often you get updates. For instance, if you get a daily update about each discussion in each of your groups, you might feel overwhelmed by the large number of emails in your inbox each day. So if you're getting too many emails more frequently than you want, change the group settings, so you don't get daily updates. Just go to "Settings" for each group, and if requested, put in your password so you can make the necessary changes.

If you don't want a daily email, uncheck "Digest Email" for each group you belong to where you don't want this email. Or to get these emails less frequently, change the frequency to once a week.

The settings page is also where you can permit members of the group to send you emails, and you can decide whether to include the group logo on your profile. Usually it's a good idea to do both to increase your visibility and accessibility to group members.

Getting Permissions from the Group Moderator

Since many groups require permission from the moderator to join, that's another reason to have a complete LinkedIn profile. Such a profile shows you are more serious and credible, so the moderator is more likely to approve your membership. A detailed profile also may suggest you are more likely to participate in group discussions, which will appeal to the group's moderator, too. So include as much information in your profile as possible to up your chances as being viewed as a valued contributor and therefore be accepted into the group.

Using the News Tab

You can use the News Tab to see what members of the group are doing and to submit your own articles. To get to the News Tab, you can open up the "Go To" menu and click "News." Or if you are already in a group, click on the "News" section under the Group Title.

Once you get to the News section, you will see a list of the latest news articles, listed by those with the most activity, those providing the latest news, or the most recently submitted, as indicated by the options on the left of the News page.

You can see a preview of each article if you put your mouse over it.

If you want to recommend an article, click the thumbs up logo, and you'll be advised that you have successfully recommended it.

Should you want to submit your own articles, simply click the "Submit a News Article" button, and enter the name of the URL where the article is located.

Then, you'll be asked to describe the article and why others should read it, such as I have done in referring readers to comments on my blog. Then, click "Submit Article", and article will immediately appear in the News section.

You can repeat the same process for each of your groups to refer people to the same article.

Using Articles to Promote Yourself

In the above demonstration, I used an article that features a topic of general interest that I have been blogging about featuring new breakthroughs in science, technology, and society called "The Very Next New Thing." But many people use articles to provide information on their field to demonstrate their expertise to appeal more directly to potential clients. For example, one marketing expert submits three articles a day to seven groups he belongs to about marketing and using the social media. Whatever your subject, posting these articles is another way to get your name out there, as well as add value to the group.

You don't have to write the articles you post yourself; you can simply post links to articles you have found valuable. For example, say you find an article in the business section of your local paper that you want to share. Just copy the link and click on "Submit New Article.

Normally, only the first 250 characters of your posting are shown, followed by a link to the article, so anyone who is interested can read more. You can also add your own summary, or if you don't write anything, LinkedIn will put in the subject for the summary of the article.

You should properly credit the source of the article, whether you wrote it or found it. You can also add a short comment to say why you posted this article or what you thought about it, such as saying "I thought this might be beneficial because it offers some great tips on how to get more traffic to your Website."

To add a comment to an article, fill out the "Add a Comment" box.

If you have written the article yourself, emphasize how it might help the group member or skip adding a comment to avoid coming across as too self-promotional.

Getting Your Name Out There by Submitting Articles

As you can see in the above posting, an advantage of posting an article is that your name and photos goes next to it, so people will see that you have submitted that article. Then, if they scroll over your name, that will take them to your profile -- another good reason to have a very complete profile.

The advantage of submitting articles often or on a daily basis is that more and more people will see your name, which builds your presence and credibility and can lead to clients and sales.

Chapter 5: Making Connections with Members

A big advantage of belonging to as many groups as possible is that this helps you connect personally with members of these groups. Otherwise, you might not be able to connect with them, because you don't know them personally or don't have a personal introduction to them.

Also, if you belong to the same group as the person you hope to connect with, if you send a message asking for permission to connect, commonly that person will invite you to send your request or send you an invitation him or herself. Plus, you can send messages to other group members, whether you are connected to them or not.

Viewing the Members of a Group

To find the members of a group to connect with, once you are in a group, go to the "More" Tab and click on "Members." Once you do, this will open up a list of all group members and indicate the number of people in the group.

Your own membership listing will appear first, followed by the people with a direct or 1st level connection to you, indicated by the number "1". If you scroll down, you will see those people with a number "2", who are your second level connections.

This second level can be quite long, since these are all people to whom your first level people are connected. Say you have 10 connections who are members of this group, and they each average 10 connections. That'll mean you will have 100 second level connections within the group.

Also notice that for each member, the number of their first level connections is listed next to their name and at the far right of their name there is a blue circle, which is filled in to reflect the number of connections -- the more connections, the more lines in the circle, until there are several hundred or more connections. The number under the "Thumbs Up" symbol indicates the number of recommendations that person has.

Connecting with the Members of a Group

While you are only linked to the 2nd level members of your group through a direct 1st level connection, you can seek to connect to them directly in one of three ways.

1) You can directly invite that person to connect with you.

2) You can send that person a message to ask for permission to send them an invitation to connect with you or ask if they would like to invite you to connect.

3) You can ask the person on your first level to introduce you to the person to whom they are connected.

• **Making a Direct Connection**

To try to connect with each person directly, click on that person's name, such as in the example below where I have selected Monique Squires, who I work with in a business connecting writers to publishers and agents, as an example.

Once you click on that person's name, this will open up that person's profile.

This profile will show you how you are connected to that person, whether it's by a single connection or many, which means that more than one person you know knows that person.

You can contact each person directly by seeking to add that person to your network by clicking "Add _____ to Your Network". Once you do this, you will get a message asking how you know that person -- as a colleague, classmate, doing business together, friend, group member, or other, in which case you will be asked to put in that person's email address. Or if you don't know that person yet, you can indicate that, too. You can also add a personal message to replace or add to the standard message that's already there: "I'd like to add you to my professional network on LinkedIn." Or you can use that. After that you'll see the name you have associated with this profile, though you can change it. Then, once you are ready to extend the invitation, click "Send Invitation."

If you use this direction connection feature, it's best to only send invites to people you know well, since they are most likely to accept. You want to invite those who are likely to accept, since when you first send out invites, you initially don't need to enter a person's email address if that person is a colleague, classmate, friend or business partner. However, if a person you invite responds that they don't know you, you will be asked to enter an email address with future invitations. This feature is designed to prevent people from spamming everyone in a group they don't know with an invitation to connect. Also, if you send too many requests to connect to people who respond that they don't know you, you risk getting dropped from the group or from LinkedIn for spamming other members.

Once you say you know someone, you'll be asked to explain how you know that person and in what capacity. Say you indicate you did business together, what company were you in?

After you send off the invitation successfully, you'll get a response back that: "Your invitation was sent successfully."

If you need to enter the person's email, you'll be asked to supply it before the invitation gets sent.

- **Inviting a Person to Connect with You**

If you don't know some directly or have only a passing acquaintance, a better approach is to send that person a message asking for that person's permission to connect or invite that person to send an invitation to connect to you. This avoids the problem of sending too many connection requests to people who respond that they don't know you. To do so, click on "Send a Message," which will open up a screen where you can write a subject line indicating what the message is about and then include your message. Then, click on "Send Message" to send it, "Cancel" if you decide not to do so.

In some cases, you'll be asked to include your email and password for the account before the message goes out to verify you are the account holder; in other cases, the message will simply be sent. In either case, once you the message goes out, you'll get a message that your message was successfully sent.

- **Asking One of Your Direct Connections to Introduce You to One of Their Connections**

Another way to add connections is to ask one of your direct connections to introduce you to someone they are connected to. However, this can be a time consuming process, because they have to take the time to contact the person you want to meet and they may not do so, or you may have to wait a long time for them to make the introduction. Thus, it can be better to use one of the other approaches, such as asking a person for his or her permission to connect, so you don't have to wait for someone to make the introduction.

Increasing Your Chances of Making a Successful New Connection

To increase your chances of a person wanting to connect with you, don't talk about yourself. Commonly, people who are active in LinkedIn will get many connection requests from people who only talk about themselves and their products or services. But that's a real turn-off, because people don't want a hard sell. Instead, make your offer to connect about the other person, such as by saying why you are interested in what that person is doing and how you might help them.

Also, be selective in who you seek to connect with, since you can only send out 3,000 connection requests. So treat connection requests carefully, and as you can, ask the other person to send a connection request to you. For instance, if you notice the person you want to connect with only has a small number of connections -- say only 70 -- you know he or she has a lot of connection request to spare. So in your message, invite that person to send you a connection request.

Additionally, when you invite someone to connect with you, it helps to mention the groups you both belong to or mention something about his or her profile to show you sincerely want to connect with that person -- he or she is not just another number to you.

Finding Out if the People You Know Are on Linked In and Inviting Them to Connect

LinkedIn can help you add people you already know to LinkedIn, using several methods featured on the Home page of your account.

Connecting with Colleagues and Classmates

One way to add connections is to find people who are already on LinkedIn who are colleagues or classmates. Just click the "Colleagues" tab to see your colleagues, including the names of people who are in your email box. You will first learn how many colleagues of yours are already members of LinkedIn. Once you click the "View" tab, you'll see a list of those you may know, so you can invite them to connect with you on LinkedIn.

Similarly, if you click on the "Classmates" tab, you can identify people you went to school with and might invite to connect with you. You will then see a list for each school you attended for either your graduation year or for all the years you attended. For example, I have 1215 contacts for the year I graduated from U.C. Berkeley in 1976. You have the option of inviting any of those classmates. However, since it is likely you won't know most of them, you might start with those you do know and invite them directly. With the others, you might ask for permission to connect, noting that you went to the same school in your message.

Once you decide to send an invitation, you'll get the following screen to write your message, along with a warning to only send invitations to people you know. To illustrate, I clicked on my own name rather than sending an invitations to people I don't know. After you send the invitation, you'll get a message indicating your invitation was successfully sent and asking if you want to send another invitation.

Adding Connections

Another way to add connections is to go to the "Add Connections" tab, which will invite you to see the people you already know on LinkedIn by entering your own email address or importing your desktop email contacts in Outlook, Apple Mail or other applications (a dialogue box that is also on your LinkedIn home page). Or you can enter the email addresses of each person you know who you would like to invite.

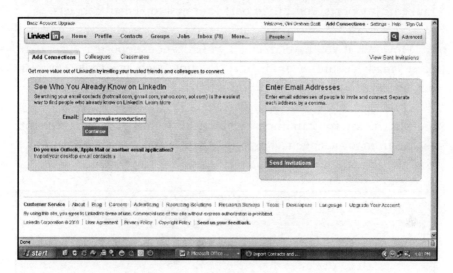

For example, I've entered some of my own email addresses below. Once you click "Send Invitation," you'll get a message that you have successfully sent out these invitations, or in my case: "You have successfully sent 3 invitations." You will then get the same screen again, inviting you to send more email invitations or see who you already know on LinkedIn.

- **Inviting the People You May Know**

Another way to make more connections is to respond to LinkedIn's suggestions on the side listing the People You May know and indicating their connection to you, such as if they are 2nd, or even 3rd level connections, who are connected to your 2nd level connections. Then, you can invite them directly or ask for permission to connection, as described earlier.

If you click, "See More," you will see even more suggestions of people you may know.

- **Inviting People in Your Own Email Accounts**

Another way to add connections is to search your own email for people you might invite. You simply put in your email, and if it is an email that LinkedIn supports, you can import your desktop email contacts.

However, if you have an email which is not supported, such as an older email account or proprietary account, such as att.net, comcast. net, or pacbell.net, you can't do this.

But let's say you can import your emails from a particular account, such as from my changemakersproductions@yahoo.com account. Once you hit continue, you will get a message to sign into your account.

Then you will be asked to grant permission to connect to LinkedIn. Once you do, everyone in your address book will be listed, and the listing will indicate whether they are already in LinkedIn or not, and you can decide who you want to connect with.

Since these people are already in my address book, once I select them, LinkedIn will automatically send them invitations, and I don't have to say how we are connected.

To send invitations to everyone, check "Select All", or choose who to invite selectively. After you send any invitations, you will be advised you have sent them out successfully and will be invited to send out additional invitations, such as when I sent out two invitations and got this message: "You have successfully sent 2 invitations." Then I had the opportunity to invite additional contacts. Each time LinkedIn suggests people you know, it lists different people.

If you have multiple emails, you can go through this process for all of your emails. For example, after advising me that I successfully sent 2 invitations, LinkedIn invited me to put in another email address to access that address book.

- **Inviting People from Webmail and Other Applications**

You can also invite people you might already be connected with through Webmail or other applications. If you click "Import Desktop Email Contacts," you will get a dialog box inviting you to upload a contacts file from an email application like Outlook, Apple Mail and others. As long as the file formats are in .csv, .txt, or .vcf formats, you can upload them.

If you want to learn more about how this works, LinkedIn will provide you with details on how to export a CSV file from Outlook, a Palm Desktop, or from ACT!. It will also tell you how to export a vCard file from a Palm Desktop or a Mac OS X Address Book.

- **Using Outlook with Linked In**

If you use Outlook, LinkedIn has an Outlook tool you can download, so you can add a LinkedIn bar on your Outlook. Then, you can invite all the people in your Outlook account to join you on LinkedIn.

Chapter 6: Starting Your Own Group

Besides joining other groups, creates you can start your own. This is an ideal way to support your business or whatever you want to promote through the group. When you have your own group, you can do things that members of a group can't do, such as inviting people to join or removing people from the group. You can also see all of the members of the group, and you can choose other administrators to help you manage the group, such as by sending out announcements for you.

How to Create a Group

To create a group, follow some simple instructions on forming a group. To begin, click on the "Create a Group" tab in the Group section, which will open up the following dialog box.

If you have a logo, use that. Browse for the logo file on your computer and upload it in a PN, JPEG, or GIF format, with a maximum size of 100 KB.

Select a name for the group and set up the group type, noting if it is an alumni, corporate, conference, networking, nonprofit, professional, or other type of group. In the later case, add your own category.

Then, briefly describe the group and its purpose. The summary will appear in the Groups Directory, while your complete description will appear on the page for that group.

You can add a Website for the group if you have one. Then, set the Group Owner's email, which may be the email you already have for the account or use another email. You can decide whether to grant open access to anyone on LinkedIn and whether to include the group in the Group's Directory, which means anyone seeking for that type of group can find it.

If you don't want an open group, uncheck the Open Access box to make the group private. You can allow group members to display their logos on their profiles or not, and you can pre-approve members if they come from a certain domain, such as if you are inviting people from a particular company or organization to join the group.

Besides designating a particular language for the group if it's other than English, which is the default, you can specify if the group is for individuals in a certain location other than the United States (the default again). You can even limit members to a certain zip code.

Finally, check that you agree to the Terms of Service and click "Create Group."

Once you create a group successfully, you will be invited to send invitations to people you want to join your group, designated by the name you selected. You can send these invitations in a batch to any individuals you have in a file of emails or to your contacts in or outside of LinkedIn.

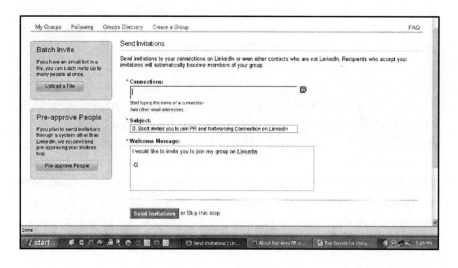

Your newly created group will show up in your list of groups, and you can edit the order in which your groups are displayed, so this comes up first, as I did so the group I just created -- the PR and Networking Connection -- comes first.

If you skip the step of inviting people after starting the group, LinkedIn will take you to the Overview box , where you can start a discussion or add a news article if you want.

Later, you can create a discussion or enter a new article at any time by going to the Discussion or News tab at the top of the group's title bar.

Creating a Discussion

As a group moderator, you can not only start a discussion and invite others to join in, but you can feature the discussion by clicking "Make this discussion featured." This means this discussion will show up on the top of the other discussions until you opt to feature another discussion. Besides featuring your own discussions, you can feature the discussions initiated by others, such as discussions you find especially interesting or those started by members you feel close to.

To begin the discussion, put in the Topic or Question you want to discuss. You can then add Additional Details if you want, as I have done in starting a discussion on "How Can You Use LinkedIn to Promote Your Company or Yourself." Then, this new discussion will show up on your Discussions page. If it's a featured discussion, you'll see the designation "Featured discussion" before the topic is listed. If you have added additional details, that will show up under the topic title. Should you make a mistake in entering this information, such as writing "Used" instead of "Use", you have 15 minutes to make changes.

Once a discussion is started, others can make comments. If you have indicated that you want to "Follow this discussion," you will be notified by email when others comment.

Adding News Articles and News Feeds

Another benefit of having a group is you can not only add news articles, like any group member, but you can add news feeds.

Submitting News Articles

Submitting a news article works just the way it does if you are a member. After you click on "Submit a news article," you will be asked to insert the Article URL. LinkedIn will then insert the title of the article and the first 250 characters for you.

After linking to an article, a good comment might be why people should read that article or your opinion about it. Once you click to "Add News Article", it will show up in the News Discussion for that group. If you click on "Latest News", you'll see your article listed there:

Adding News Feeds

As a group moderator, you can add news feeds by clicking on "Manage news feeds," as an alternative to copying and pasting articles into the news. To do so, enter the name of a Website or an RSS URL. You can enter your own Website if you want, or you can feature a feed that is relevant for your group. You can include up to 30 feeds.

For example, if you are especially interested in featuring news about the social media, you might add "Mashable" into the "Add a News Feed" box. Then, you will get a link to those feeds.

Once you click on "Add News Feeds", you will be advised that the feed or feeds you selected have been successfully added, and you can add another feed. It may take up to an hour to start seeing these feeds appear under the Latest News, and then the feeds will be automatically updated at least once every 6 hours.

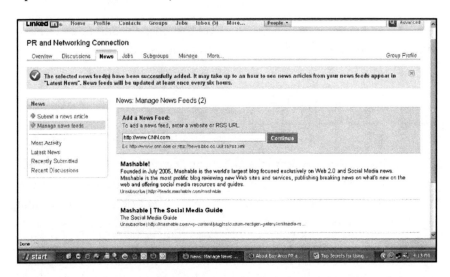

These news feeds will combine any articles from the feed with the articles you select. For instance, a news article from my blog is listed first as a featured article, and then over 100 articles are listed that come from the CNN feed.

If you do have news feeds for your group, this is a good reason to feature the news articles you or your group members send in, so they will go to the top of the list.

You can also select the news articles that have generated the most interest, if you click on "Most Activity."

If you go to an established group, you will see the news articles grouped by those which have had the most activity based on the number of views and comments. As your own group builds up and there is more activity, a similar pattern will emerge as people start following the news articles you post or which come in through a news feed.

Managing Your Members

Besides inviting members to join, you can remove and block members from your group. A reason to do so is if someone is being disruptive or only using the group to promote their own products or services. You can delete any content they submit which you object to, as well. Go to the Manage tab, search for the name of the member you want to remove or block, and click the "Remove", "Remove and Block," or "Remove, Block, and Delete Contributions" button.

Sending Announcements

As manager of your group, you can send out announcements to everyone by going to Manage and clicking "Sending an Announcement." You can send one announcement per week. At one time, LinkedIn allowed moderators to download an email list of all the people in their group, but they stopped doing that to prevent spam. Even so, if you have a large group, say 50,000 people, you can send an announcement to all of these people once a week through LinkedIn. These announcements are ideal if you have trainings, events, new products or services, or special news to announce.

Creating Subgroups

When your group grows, subgroups are a way to invite members into smaller groups that share a special interest. Click "Create a Subgroup", fill in the same sort of information as in creating the group. Then, you can invite everyone in your group to join or invite individuals selectively.

Part II: Finding What You Want Through Searches and Questions

Chapter 7: Using Search to Find Contacts and Information

Search is a powerful tool for finding new prospects or clients. You can search in groups or generally. If you are a member of a group, you can send people messages directly whether you are connected with them or not. If you are not connected to someone and do a general search, you can still potentially connect with that person by sending them an invite. However, it is best not to send someone you don't know an invite directly; rather, go through some additional steps to connect with them, as will be described, due to the dangers of being rejected and possibly being considered a spammer.

The Search Box is on the top right of your home page, where it says People, which is the default.

You can search by people, companies, jobs, answers, your inbox, or by groups.

Doing a General Search

If you do a general search by People and start typing in a letter or name, LinkedIn will show you up to 10 people or companies who share that letter, combination of letters, or names.

The names of the people who show up are those you are connected to, since you can only see the names of people in your network (which includes your first, second, or third level connections) or in your groups. (You can tell which they are by the 1, 2, or 3 in the circle next to each person's name). But the company names will appear whether you have a connection with anyone in that company or not, as long as the company has a profile on LinkedIn. For example, when I type in the letters "so," I get a mix of names of individuals and companies.

Once an individual or company name is in your Search Box, you can go to that individual's or company's profile to learn more about them. Just click on that person's or company's name.

Or if you put in the name of that company, you can go to that company's profile and see the different people who work there, including the high level officers. If you have a connection to someone there through your network, you will see their name and their connection to you (1st, 2nd, 3rd, or a member of one of your groups). Otherwise, you will just see that person's title.

For instance, say I put the name "Universal" in the Search Box and see a list of companies with that name.

Then, if I click on Universal Studios, I will see a list of all their employees, starting with their current employees and their past employees who are part of my network -- in this case, second level contacts who I am connected with through someone else. Additionally, it lists the new hires and popular profiles, even though I have no connection to them. However, if I try to look more extensively at the list of current employees by clicking "See more," I will only see those employees by name who are in my network, and the others by title only, such as in the example below.

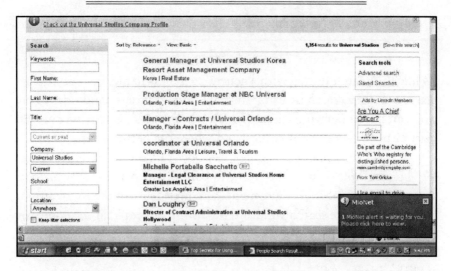

But even if you have no direct connection with a person and just have a job title, if you already know some people in the company, that could help you contact the person you don't know. For example, you could mention who you already know there, when you contact the person you haven't met yet to open up a dialogue. Depending on the company, you might be able to connect with top level managers, vice-presidents, and even the president or CEO.

You may be amazed at the people you are already connected to at a company.

If you click, "See more," you'll see even more people you are connected to, starting with your first, then your second, and finally your third level connections and any individuals with whom you share a group membership, as in the examples below. The number next to each name indicates the type of connection you have. Since Universal has over 1300 employees listed and over 500 current employees, a huge number of connections are possible.

But you can only see up to 100 of these connections, 10 per page, with a basic subscription. To see more, you have to upgrade to one of the premium subscriptions.

Doing a More Targeted Search

While this search started with a general search by name, you can further narrow down a search by using the boxes along the left hand side, where you can put in keywords, a first or last name, a title, whether a current, past or both types of employees, and where the person lives.

For example, if you only want to connect with the vice-presidents at a company or above, you can put "vice president" in the Keywords or Title box, and the search will limit the listing of people in the company to that.

The listing will include anyone in your network through your personal or group connections by name, so you can contact them directly. To contact them, click on their name; then you can send them a message, get introduced by a closer connection if they are 2nd or 3rd level connections, ask to add them to your network, or find references who might be able to introduce you.

If you want to send a message, you'll get the usual message screen, and you can add an additional 49 people if you want to send everyone the same message. As previously noted, such messages are a good way to either ask someone for permission to connect or invite the person to send you an invitation to connect. In either case, explain why you want to make the connection.

If you want to get introduced, you can send that person a message asking to be connected through someone you both know. You can indicate the reason for the introduction, using the LinkedIn menu.

Also, you can include a personal message to the person you both know in common.

However, you can only send out 5 of these introductions at a time if you have a personal LinkedIn account, though you can send out more with a premium account.

You can send out a direct invitation to connect, indicating how you know this person, though for reasons already discussed, unless you do already have some connection, it is best not to send a direct invitation, since if you get too many of these invites rejected, your account might be limited or suspended for spamming.

Searching for References

Should you be interested in working with or for someone or hiring someone, you can do a search for references, which is designed to give you more information about potential employees, employers, or business partners. To start the search, under "People," go to "Advanced Search." Then, go to "References Search." You can then enter the name the name of a company where you are interested in obtaining references.

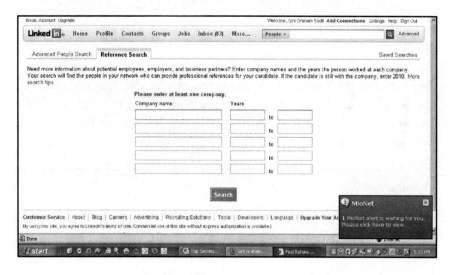

However, to get a list of these potential references to contact them directly through inMail, you have to upgrade your account to a Business or Pro account by clicking Upgrade Now. Doing so costs $25 to $500 a month, depending on how many messages you want to send out. You can send out these messages without having an introduction, as well as view the profiles of over 60 million professionals at 200,000 plus companies, though you have no connection to them through your network.

An alternative approach is to do a search by the company to see if you already have connections there, who you contact directly. Or if you have no connection to a person through your network, you will just see their title.

Should you want to contact that person directly, you can use Inmail, but have to upgrade your account to do so by clicking Upgrade.

You also have to upgrade your account if you want to see the name or full profile or send that person an email, when you only have someone's title. You cannot get introduced to that person directly, because they are not in your network.

Searching for Work

You can also use LinkedIn to search for jobs by selecting for "Jobs" in the Search Box. If you just click in the box, you'll get a listing of jobs anywhere. But if you click in the Advanced Job Search Box, you can narrow down your options.

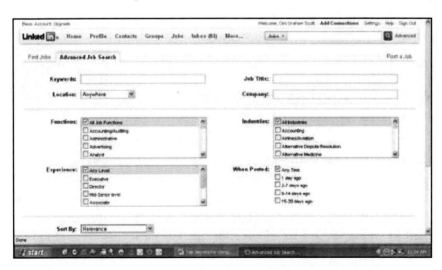

You can limit your search to jobs in your area, since your zip code is entered automatically, or if you want to find a job somewhere else, change the zip code. Then, put in a keyword to indicate the type of job you are looking for.

You can narrow or extend your search to look for jobs closer or further away by changing the number of miles on the "Within" tab.

If you want to apply for a job, you can check if anyone in your network already works there, since you can use that person as a reference. The listing will show everyone from 1st to 3rd level and those in groups with you.

When you click on the name of the company with the job listing, you will see additional information about the job, and you can apply for it online. In addition, you will see information about other jobs at that company at the end of the listing, as well as suggestions for similar jobs in other companies. In some case, you may find that the company is particularly interested in people who already have recommendations, and they can check on your profile to see the number of recommendations you already have -- another reason to get recommendations from others.

When you apply for a job, you will get an application form for the company which you can fill out and submit. Each company will indicate the information they want and how you should apply. While some companies will ask for you to apply with detailed information online, such as Google's application asking for educational background, employment history, resume, and other information, other companies may just ask you to provide some basic information and write a cover letter.

If you use the Advanced Job Search, you can narrow your search even more, and you can even look for a job in a particular company. You can also note the particular fields you are interested in, how far you want to go for the job, the kind of work you want to do and so forth.

If the response you get in your job search is too limited, you can see more jobs from Simply Hired that fit your criteria. Once you find any job that is of interest, you can see a list of contacts in your network who can help you get that job. Just click on "See who at (that company) can help you get the job." You may be amazed at the number of connections you have as you go down through the levels of your network.

If you have a job you are offering to hire someone, you can post that, though there is a charge to post a job -- $195 for a 30 day listing, though there is no charge for the job search. You enter the Job Title, the Location, the Company URL, the Type of job, the Experience you are looking for, the Industry you are in and other relevant information you want from a job candidate.

Searching for Companies and People in Companies

You can also search for people in particular companies. Select "Companies" in the Search Box, and if you click the button to do a general search, you'll get a list of all the companies where you have a 1st or 2nd level connection. For example, I have over 100,000 results, which is pretty amazing, considering I have only 268 first level connections.

Then, you can limit your search by company name, industry, location, company size, and whether that company is currently hiring, using the boxes on the left.

Alternatively, you can broaden your search, because LinkedIn will suggest related industries. Once I add those, there are over 59,000 results.

If you put in the name of a particular company, you will get not only that company, but its branches and affiliates.

When you click on the company's name, you will see its current employees, starting with those in your network, then former employees, new hires, recent promotions and changes, as in the Universal Studios example described before.

However, you will only see the names of the people in your network and just the job titles of the others, aside from the lists of new hires, recent promotions and changes, and popular profiles. But you can still send anyone, whether you are connected to them or not, an InMail, if you have a premium account, as previously noted in the discussion of searching for people generally.

The advantage of this company search feature is that you can focus on particular industries or on companies within certain locations and seek to contact people you want to meet in those companies by getting introductions and references or by sending InMails.

Searching for Groups and People in Groups

You can search for groups and for people in the groups you already belong to, so you can contact them. You can start with a general search and then narrow down your search using keywords. This search function also links to the Groups category in LinkedIn, discussed in Chapter 2.

Searching for Groups

A general search is a good way to find groups to join. Go to Search and look for groups in your area of interest. If you don't narrow down your search, you will get a list of all the groups in LinkedIn -- currently about 540,000 of them.

Though there is no advanced search function when you go to the groups tab in the Search Box as there is for people, you can narrow down your search by category. These categories include alumni, corporate, conference, networking, nonprofit, and professional groups. Also, you can put in keywords to select particular types of groups, such as "film," "writing," and "real estate."

By using keywords or categories, you will get a more targeted list of groups. The more keywords you put in, the more you will narrow your search, since the group will need to contain all of these words.

The groups that turn up in your search are listed by size, with the largest group first, then the next largest, and so on.

If you are already a member of certain groups, LinkedIn will indicate you are "Already a member." Otherwise, you will have the option to "Join this group." You can scroll down to see additional groups and find groups to join this way, though you can further narrow your search by doing an advanced search.

Once you indicate your interest, you will have various options, such as whether to display the group's logo on your profile and what email organizers should use. Also, you can indicate whether you want a daily digest, want group announcements, or want people in the group to send you messages (though they won't be able to see your email).

Once you ask to join the group, you will get a notice that you have requested to join that group. Your request will then go to the group organizer.

You can join any number of groups at a time.

Then, you have to wait for the organizer to review your request and decide whether or not to approve it. The group organizer may look at your profile, other group memberships, recommendations, and other factors to decide whether to accept you into the group.

Your notice about your request to join will list the groups where you are currently a member. If you are a member of a number of groups, you can edit the order in which they are displayed. Click "Edit the order of your groups" to do so, and you will see the list of groups with numbers next to their names indicating their rank in the list. You can move the groups up or down using the up and down arrow keys or change the numbers. When you change the numbers, any group with the same number will be pushed down to the next lower position.

You can indicate how many groups up to 10 that you want to show in the main navigation section for your groups. The groups you have asked to join will be listed at the end as pending.

If you want to change the settings of any group you belong to, click on the "Member Settings" next to that group. Then the settings dialogue box for that group will appear, so you can change the settings.

Searching for People in Groups

Once you are a member of a group, you can search for other members of that group by going to "Members."

That member search will give you a list of the people who are members of that group, which you can review. You can then further search for people who are members of that group. The members on your first level (1st) are listed first after your own name; then those on your second level (2nd) are listed after that to the end of all your connections or up to 500 listings in that group, such as in my listing of members in the Film TV Connection.

The membership listing will indicate who has recently joined the group in the last 7 days, indicated on the left under "New Members: Last 7 Days."

You can also look for members of the group who have certain jobs or titles by using keywords.

A good way to narrow your search is to include the location, as well as the type of person in the industry you are targeting. Then you can narrow that down even further by noting a particular city. While some of people may be listed for other locations, they will also include the indicated words in their profiles.

You can also click on "Advanced Search" in the group or in a number of groups, which will give you various options for targeting your search. You can opt to include your first or second connections or all group members in that group, in other selected groups, or all of your groups. You can also choose all companies or selected companies; all locations or selected locations (which indicates the numbers of members in each location); the industry (which shows all related industries), the previous companies the person worked for; the schools members have attended; the person's language; and when they joined LinkedIn.

The Industry and Groups categories indicate how many people are in different groups, with the group where you started the search highlighted. If you are interested in connecting with someone who attended a particular school, you can select that, too, as well as the person's language and when they joined.

For example, say I limit my search to film professionals who are only in the film and motion picture industry. I will get only 68 connections if I only include my first and second level connections. But if I include my group member connections, I will get an additional 133 connections, for a total of 159 connection. So that illustrates the importance of belonging to groups -- so you can connect with people you aren't otherwise connected to.

Connecting with High Level People

You can also use LinkedIn to connect with high level people in an industry if they are members, as well as with regular employees, through your connections with other members or through groups. Being a member of a group is especially important if you are new to LinkedIn and have not yet built up your network.

Say you want to connect with current employees who are at least vice-presidents at Universal. You would start by putting "Universal" in the Search Box, starting with the Companies tab.

Then, from the list of companies you get, pick out the company you want to contact, such as Universal Pictures. You will then see all the current and former employees, plus recent hires and changes. You will also see the number of people in your network and can check if anyone in your network is at the VP level.

When you find someone at that level, you can click on their profile to see how closely they are connected to you. For example, I found a President of one of the divisions who is a third-level connection to me. Then, if you look at the recommendations for that person, you may find other high-level people you can connect to at other companies.

Once you start looking for people within a company, the Search Box will change from Company to People. Now you might check on all the people at the VP level you might connect with. In fact, you might be amazed at who you can connect to. For instance, when I did this, I found that I had a 2nd level connection to President Barack Obama!

But to go back to reality. Say you want to look for all the VPs in a company. Look for the Current Employees section, then click on "See more." You will then see a list of current employees, starting with your highest level contacts.

If you put "vice president" in the search field, that will indicate who in the company is a vice president and your connections to them. The company name will already be in the Search Box, so you are only searching for VPs in that company. When I did this at Universal, I found 53 VPs who were part of the company. The ones in my network, including many who were in one of my groups, are listed by name; or if the VCs are not connected to me, they are just listed by title. If you share multiple groups, LinkedIn will list the number of groups you share together.

You can then strategically decide who to contact, based on what you want to promote -- an event, a script, a product, a musical act, or a service. Besides looking for those with relevant job titles, look for those who are as close as possible and contact them first, then those with whom you share the most groups. You can use your connections to help you in gaining entry to that high level person to whom you are not yet connected.

However, whether you are looking for a business connection or work, it is best to establish a connection request and start a relationship first, before doing any self-promotion. Focus on what you might be able to do to help that person, rather than what he or she can do to help you. Later, after you establish the connection, you can try to get what you are looking for.

The Advantage of Being in Groups in Doing a Search

Because of the way searching works, you will see many more contacts when you have group memberships than if you are just looking for 1st, 2nd, or 3rd level connections. Also, when you do a search for members in groups, you can see up to 25 pages of members with 20 per page, or up to 500 members. If you weren't in a group, and you do an advanced search, you will only see 10 pages with 10 individuals per page.

For example, if you do a general search of people who are film producers, you will discover there are 3861 results -- but you can only see the first 100 with 10 per page. If you try to see anymore, you'll be invited to upgrade your account to a premium account, where you can see 300 to 700 more at a time, depending on the monthly payment for your account.

If you do a search in your own groups and to people with a 1st or 2nd level connection, you can limit the search for people who are more targeted and to whom you are more closely connected.

You still can only see 100 people with a basic account, but you could try parsing your search to see more people through a series of searches. For example, while I only have two 1st level connections, I have 232 2nd level connections; 833 group members for all groups; and 105 for a selected group, the Film and TV Professionals.

In other words, if you get creative, you can limit your search in various ways, so you can see the most relevant members of your different groups.

Searching for People in a Selected Area

If you want to promote something in a particular area, you can do that looking for people who have a certain city in their profile or within a certain distance from a selected zip code. For example, say you want to search for people who have Los Angeles in their profile. You would put in an L.A. zip code, such as 90401, which is the code for Santa Monica. Without any other filters, there would be 325,282 people within 10 miles.

To make it larger, within 100 miles, it's 1,772,525 people, within 25 miles, it's 882,613.

You can further limit the connections if you get a large number of people in a big city. One good way is to narrow it down to the people who are only your 1st or 2nd connections. For instance, when I do that, within 10 miles there are only 5915 connections; 53 with only my first level connections.

If you still have a very large group, you can further limit it by targeting a particular industry. You can tell how many are in each industry by the number next to the listing. For example, if I target the motion picture and film industry, I will see 532 connections at my 1st and 2nd level

You can limit it still more if you put in a particular job title. For instance, when I put in producer there are 254 producers on my 1st and 2nd level within 10 miles of Santa Monica

In short, you can target people in your network in your area as close as 10 miles away to 100 miles. And you can continually narrow down the number of people by adding in additional filters, such as the industry and whether they are your 1st or 2nd level contacts. To be even more specific, you might limit your search to a particular town or city by including that in the keywords or by selecting a zip code from the Location box for a particular metro area.

If you aren't sure what zip code to use, click the "Lookup" link, next to the Postal Code box.

Then you can put in the name of the targeted city as your starting point. For example, if you put in Santa Monica, you will get a half-dozen possible zip codes. Chose one to enter into the Postal Code box -- and if you are not sure which one to use, choose the first one, which is likely to be the main post office or downtown area.

Searching for Names
or Subjects in Your Inbox

LinkedIn can help you search by the names of people or by subject in your LinkedIn Inbox. So if you have a lot of mail, this can be a way to target what you are looking for. This is also a way to pull up your mail to and from a particular person.

You can search directly from your Inbox. Or you can put in the name or subject you are lookiing for in the Search Box. If you put your search term in the Search Box on top, it will automatically be repeated in the box on the left, though if you put the word in the box on the left it won't be repeated on top.

For a more precise search, put your term or terms "in quotes". Otherwise, you will get back items that have each word individually.

When you do a name search, it will pick up the name of that person within your email as well as someone to whom you have sent an email or who has responded to your email.

If you want to pull up emails about a discussion on a particular topic, put that keyword in either box. If your initial search using two words is too specific, just use one word to broaden the search. For instance, when I put in "film producer," I only found 3 emails, but when I put in "producer," over a dozen emails turned up. If I didn't use quotes, I got a much larger number of responses, since LinkedIn included emails that mentioned "film" or "producer" in any way.

Chapter 8: Finding Answers and Asking Questions

If you are looking for information or want to pose questions yourself, LinkedIn can help you through its "Answers" feature. You can also use both answers and questions to promote your business or yourself by answering questions with your expertise, or posing questions that others have and answering them with helpful information.

I'll first focus on using LinkedIn to search for answers from already asked questions or questions you ask. Then, I'll discuss using your questions and answers to promote your business or yourself by building relationships and showing your expertise.

Searching for Answers

To search for answers to your questions, go to "Answers" in the Search Box or the More menu.

These are two main ways of getting to the Answers function, so you can look for already asked questions and answers, get answers, answer questions yourself, and pose your own questions.

When you use Search to find answers, without putting in a particular topic, you'll see the questions sorted by the ones asked by your closest connections on LinkedIn. But these questions could have been asked some time ago. To see the most recent questions, sort them by date. You can see the questions asked even a few seconds ago.

To search by relevance, ask a question about a subject or put in a few keywords. You'll get back answers which include or are related to the subject or keywords. You can also search by Questions with Answers, Questions Only, or Unanswered Questions. Besides finding answers, searching for questions is a way to find ones you can answer to show your expertise in that topic. You will see up to 500 responses, 10 per page.

For example, to find out more about the social media or respond to questions in this field, put "social media" in the Keywords box. If you sort any questions by relevance, you'll get responses based on the number of answers to the question, with the largest first. If you sort by date, you'll get the most recent responses.

Unless you limit questions to individuals in your network or group, questions can be posed by anyone on LinkedIn. But if a question is posed by someone outside your network, this can be a good way to add people to your network. To do so, click on the person's name to go to his or her profile. Then, you can ask to add that person to your network or send an InMail.

If you click on the question, you'll see what the person asked, which may include an expanded description about the question, and sometimes their own answer to the question, since some people ask a question to show off their expertise and get feedback from others.

To see all of the questions and answers a person has posed or given, click on "see all my questions."

If you scroll down you'll see the answers and the name of the person posting an answer. You can see all of that person's questions and answers by clicking "see all my answers."

While these questions and answers sorted by relevance or date can be answered by anyone on LinkedIn, if people are in your network, you'll see their level indicated by the number next to their name.

If you want to see the questions your network connections are asking on a topic, sort by "Degrees away from you." You'll see their questions and answers listed with your 1st degree contacts first. While you may know many of these people personally, some of their questions may be from months or even years ago. For example, the questions that popped up when I checked on the questions and answers posted by a friend were from about 6-18 months ago.

So it's better to sort by date to get the latest questions and responses.

You can also zero in on more recent questions, whether you check by date, relevance, or from network connections if you look at Open Questions. For example, a search for questions about the social media led to 177 open questions, though these are sorted in three different ways --by date, relevance, and those in my social network.

To do a more specific search for answers, go to the Advanced Answers Search.

When you do an Advanced Search for answers, you can put in selected keywords and target a particular category, such as startups and small businesses, and further limit the search to only small businesses.

For all questions targeted by date, there are 440 questions; for open questions, only 7 questions.

To answer a question, zero in on the most recent questions raised on a topic of interest. Then, this might be a way to introduce yourself to or get to know the people who respond favorably to your answer.

Picking out topics to answer where you are knowledgeable can also be a way to find potential clients who can benefit from what you know or who you know as an expert in that field. For example, in response to a question about how a small business can do their own PR, you can answer it directly if you are involved in the PR field or if not, perhaps you might suggest a friend or business associate to answer it. And then, perhaps that might lead to some business for your friend or associate that might turn into a referral back to you -- a principle followed in many business referral networks, where people share leads with one another.

To recommend an expert, click "Suggest Expert." Then, you can indicate who you are suggesting and write a little about why that person is an expert on this topic. If you are suggesting someone not in your network, you can include a name and Website or email, so the questioner can contact that person directly. If you suggest someone from your network, a list of everyone in your network will pop up, and you can select up to three people to recommend.

Besides providing an answer yourself, you can suggest your associates or company as an outside expert. For example, after I provided some advice about doing PR, I included my Websites for individuals who want to know more -- and possibly use my services. Similarly, when you answer, think how to provide value in your answer before promoting your own services. This way you don't just advise people to "hire me," but you provide other options without you. But the useful information you provide might make others want to hire you.

Once you hit "Submit," you will be advised that your answer has been posted, and you can see it along with other answers to that question.

If you provide good answers, you can also gain recognition and expert points for giving the best answer to a question. Eventually, with enough points, you will earn expert status, and as an expert, you will be featured on the Answers home page and in each category of questions.

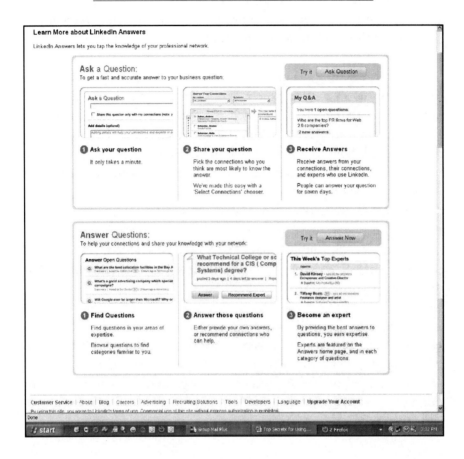

To answer more questions like the one you just answered, click on "View more questions like this one." You will then see a list of Open Questions from your network connections dealing with that topic (ie: social media and small businesses).

Thus, looking for answers can not only be a way to find answers for your questions, whether you or others ask them, giving and responding to answers can be a way to start a dialogue with others. Then, if these people aren't already in your network, you can seek to add them. As you build a relationship through your questions, the responses to them, and your own answers, you can increase trust and use the connections you make to share information on your company, products, and services.

Asking Questions

To ask a question to get answers, enter your question in the "Ask a Question" box on the Answer Home page or go to the "Ask a Question" tab.

For example, using the "Ask a Question" box, I asked the following question about how effective the social media has been in helping people get customers or clients.

Once you pose your question, it is added to the Ask a Question page; or if you go directly to the Ask a Question page, you can write your question there.

While you can choose to limit sharing your question to your connections, you will get fewer answers, so it is best to leave the "only share this question with connections I select" box unchecked. You can then add more details and further categorize your question. If your question is related to recruiting, promoting your services, or job seeking, you should mention that, since such questions are supposed to be asked privately to selected individuals or those in your network, and LinkedIn warns against miscategorizing your question, since if you do, your question might be removed or reported by other users.

You can use the "Add details" section to further explain what you want to know, such as when I noted that "I'm interested in what social media you are using and which has been most effective for you." Then, categorize your question by selecting the most relevant category in the box on the left, which will open up a more selective list in the next box. And after you select a sub-category here, you may have still other choices in the third box.

After you ask your question, it will be posted for responses for seven days, and you can additionally send it to your personal direction connections.

Once you have finishing asking your question, you will see it posted under "My Q&A".

If your question is specifically related to recruiting, looking for a job, or promoting your own services, and you check that, you will be limited to asking it of your own connections.

Once you have everything checked, click "Ask Question." You can then send your question to up to 200 connections to get answers.

You can send your question to specific connections by name, or call up your list of direct connections to send your question to up to 200. Should you have more than 200 connections, send your question to another group of up to 200 connections. To illustrate, I've chosen Monique Squires, who I work with at Publishers and Agents. Once I selected her in the box beside her name on the left, her name popped up in the message box on the right.

Once you select everyone you want to get the message, click "Finish." You'll then see the message, can add to it if you wish to personalize it, and send yourself a copy if desired.

After you click "Send," you'll see that the question has been sent to the selected recipients.

Whether you ask open or personal questions, you are limited to 10 a month. For instance, I have now asked 1open question about the social media and 3 questions about promoting my business and service which are classified as private questions. So I can only ask 6 more this month. But while you are limited in asking questions, you can keep on answering others' questions or suggesting experts to provide answers.

Becoming an Expert

Becoming an expert is a good way to increase your credibility and promote your business, since you increase awareness and gain recognition as you answer questions as a knowledgeable expert.

Each week, the experts who give the most answers get billing as This Week's Top Experts, and the numbers next to their names show how closely connected they are to you. You can see all of their answers to other questions, if you click "see all my answers."

To see even more top experts, click "more top experts," where you will find the 500 top experts listed, based on their number of questions answered.

These listings indicate the number of times each expert has given the best answers in different categories, such as in using LinkedIn, Web Development, and Computers and Software.

How do you gain expertise yourself? If you click "How do I earn expertise," you'll discover that the way to do this is by answering open questions, and every time the questioner picks your answer as the best, you'll get a point of expertise. The more points of expertise you get, the higher you will appear on LinkedIn's list of experts

So find categories where you really are an expert, answer questions, and start building up points.

Part 3: Using Applications

Chapter 9: The Top Ten Applications

The Apps I will be featuring are these:

- Company Buzz
- Word Press
- Blog Link
- Google Presentation
- SlideShare Presentations
- Events
- My Travel
- Box.net Files
- Reading List
- Polls

You will find a number of special applications if you go to "More" and click on the "Applications Directory." There are 13 of them as of this writing, and I'll discuss the ten most important ones and how to use them.

Applications FAQ Feedback Browse More Applications

LinkedIn Applications enable you to enrich your profile, share and collaborate with your network, and get the key insights that help you be more effective. Applications are added to your homepage and profile enabling you to control who gets access to what information.

Reading List by Amazon
by Amazon

Extend your professional profile by sharing the books you're reading with other LinkedIn members. Find out what you should be reading by following updates from your connections, people in your field, or other LinkedIn members of professional interest to you.

Box.net Files
by Box.net

Add the Box.net Files application to manage all your important files online. Box.net lets you share content on your profile, and collaborate with friends and colleagues.

Polls
by LinkedIn

The Polls application is a market research tool that allows you to collect actionable data from your connections and the professional audience on LinkedIn.

Blog Link
by SixApart

With Blog Link, you can get the most of your LinkedIn relationships by connecting your blog to your LinkedIn profile. Blog Link helps you, and your professional network, stay connected.

Company Buzz
by LinkedIn

Ever wonder what people are saying about your company? Company Buzz shows you the twitter activity associated with your company. View tweets, trends and top key words. Customize your topics and share with your coworkers.

Google Presentation
by Google

Present yourself and your work. Upload a .PPT or use Google's online application to embed a presentation on your profile.

SlideShare Presentations
by SlideShare Inc

SlideShare is the best way to share presentations on LinkedIn! You can upload & display your own presentations, check out presentations from your colleagues, and find experts within your network.

My Travel
by Tripit, Inc.

See where your LinkedIn network is traveling and when you will be in the same city as your colleagues. Share your upcoming trips, current location, and travel stats with your network.

Events
by LinkedIn

Find professional events, from conferences to local meet-ups, and discover what events your connections are attending.

WordPress
by WordPress

Connect your virtual lives with the WordPress LinkedIn Application. With the WordPress App, you can sync your WordPress blog posts with your LinkedIn profile, keeping everyone you know in the know.

Huddle Workspaces
by Huddle.net

Huddle gives you private, secure online workspaces packed with simple yet powerful project, collaboration and sharing tools for working with your connections.

SAP Community Bio
by LinkedIn

Display your certified SAP expertise on LinkedIn. The SAP Community Bio application allows you to add your SAP contributions and credentials to your professional profile.

Tweets
by LinkedIn

Access the most important parts of the professional conversation with Tweets, a Twitter client you can use.

As you add Apps, they will show up on your More file menu. Should you want to remove any apps, you can always do so by clicking the "remove" button next to that app.

Company Buzz

Company Buzz is a way of monitoring what people say on Twitter about your business or about any business or person for that matter on Twitter. When you click on "Company Buzz," you will see a description of how this application works and an invitation to add the application.

To add the application, click "Add Application," and if you don't uncheck "Display on LinkedIn Home Page" it will show up on your home page. To see what people are saying about your company or you, put in your company name or your own name, though if other companies or individuals have similar names, these will show up, too, such as when I did a search for "Changemakers", the name of one of my companies. Then, look for those statements, if any, which refer to your company or you.

If no one is currently saying anything or very little, you'll see that, too. For example, when I put in my full company name for this account -- Changemakers Productions, nothing appeared, and when I put in my own name, I got one hit.

You can put in any individual or company name to see what people are saying about them.

WordPress

If you have a blog using WordPress or located on the WordPress site, you can download the WordPress application to connect your post from your WordPress blog directly to your LinkedIn profile. This way anytime you publish a new WordPress post, it will show up in your LinkedIn profile in reverse chronological order, the latest first.

To put WordPress on your profile, go to More, then to the Applications Directory, and scroll down to the WordPress logo.

When you click this, you will get a screen showing you how this application will look like when you download it.

You can display this app on your profile, LinkedIn home page, or both. Say you click both. You will get a page asking you to enter the site for your blogs and ask if you want to display all recent posts or only those tagged "linkedin." The default is to include them all, which is best, unless you want to distinguish which blogs are to be shown on LinkedIn. If you don't already have a blog, you can set up a free blog on WordPress at www.wordpress.com.

To set up your WordPress blog, simply create a user name, password, and confirm that.

Once you have a blog, the application will appear on your LinkedIn home page and will feature all of your recent blogs.

Blog Link

Blog Link is an important app if you have a blog on a site other than on Word Press or want to know about the blogs that others on your network have , such as on www.myblogspot.com or www.blogger.com. You can use Blog Link to find your blog on the Internet and link it to your LinkedIn profile.

To get started, go to Blog Link in the Applications Directory and click on it.

You'll then see a brief description about it and an invitation to add the application.

Once you add it, Blog Link will search for blogs by you and people you know on your network.

For example, these are blogs by the people on my network organized by date and then alphabetically for each person with a blog for the last two days. If you haven't blogged in that time, it won't pick up a blog by you.

If you go to your home page or profile page, you will see the application with the latest blogs by people in your network or by you.

Google Presentation

With Google Presentation, you can add a PowerPoint presentation to your LinkedIn profile or link to it from your homepage. This is a good way to show what you are doing or feature some useful tips that others can use. If you can't make PowerPoint presentations on your computer, you can embed a presentation on your profile.

To add this app, go to More and to the Applications Directory to find the Google Presentation logo.

When you click on the Google Presentation logo, you'll get a screen showing how the app works. As Google explains, there are three major ways to use this application:

- Showcase a recent talk or presentation.
- Display a visual portfolio of your professional accomplishments.

- Introduce yourself to recruiters and professional contacts viewing your profile.

Indicate whether you want to show these presentations on your profile, home page, or both.

Once you sign in, Google asks you how you will present yourself and invites you to add a presentation.

You then need to sign into a Google gmail account to do this, or if you don't already have one, you can create it now.

Once you have signed into your gmail account, you can upload any file you want.

If you click Upload a Presentation, you can look for an already created PowerPoint presentation on your computer.

Once you upload the presentation, you can add it to your profile by clicking Post to Profile. Then, Google will ask you if it is okay to publish the presentation. Click okay to agree.

Then your presentation is up there as a slide show others can view.

To share this presentation with any of your connections, click the "Share this presentation with my connections" link. You will then be invited to indicate the contacts you want to share it with. Click the "in" button to bring up everyone you are connected to. Then, you can share the presentation with up to 50 contacts at a time.

After you select the individuals to send it to, you will get a message indicating who will be getting your message. If you want, you can personalize the message. Then, send it. To illustrate, I have sent a message to myself and one of my editors, explaining why I am sending this to her (Would you like to publish my LinkedIn book?). Generally, it's best not to let the people you send the message to see each other's names and email addresses. So uncheck that option but send a copy to yourself.

Once you send your invitation, you'll get a message that your message was successfully sent, as well as see your presentation again.

You can now upload another presentation. Once you have two or more presentations to show, you can select which one to share with others.

You can show up to three presentations on your Home page, Profile, or both, as indicated below. However, if the presentation is on your Home page, there will be just a small thumbnail of the first slide. To see the full presentation, viewers have to click on "View on Profile" or go to your full profile, where they can click to see each slide.

To change the presentation you are showing, click on "click here to change the presentation in your profile," which will take you back to the screen for creating a presentation. You can edit the current presentation online if you click "Edit," or you can edit your presentation on your computer if you have created it there and upload the latest version.

If you do edit it online, you can create a duplicate slide, change the copy, add images, and do most other key edits as you might normally do in PowerPoint.

Or if you create a presentation using Google's online application, click on Create Your Presentation. Then, you'll go to this screen to start creating your slides.

The Google app doesn't have all the bells and whistles that come with Microsoft's PowerPoint. While you can add a theme, text, images, and graphics, as indicated on the menu below, you are limited to a few themes, slide layouts, and text styles. Still, you can create a great looking presentation.

Here's an example of a slide which I created in a few minutes, using images from my computer. You can also import individual slides from a previously created presentation or even the whole presentation, so you could combine several presentations into one.

The program is a little clunkier and slower to work with than using Microsoft's PowerPoint, but creates a nice basic presentation. Once you've created the presentation in Google, it has it's own URL, which you can share with others in various ways.

While the Google Presentation is designed for PowerPoints, you can use it to share individual photos. Just import them into a presentation to do so.

Once you have created your online presentation, you can let people know about it in various ways: you can invite people to see it, email it as an attachment, publish and embed it, or a combination of approaches.

If you want to publish and embed it, you will then get this screen letting you know you haven't yet published your presentation and inviting you to do so by clicking "Publish document."

Once you publish your document, you will be advised where it is available for viewing as part of .doc.google.com. You will be given a code that you can paste into the html of any Website or blog, so others can see it. You can save the completed presentation to your own computer. And you can display it on your LinkedIn home page and profile. To display it on LinkedIn, download the published presentation as a PowerPoint or PDF. Then it will show up on your home page and profile.

Once you have more than one PowerPoint on your profile, you can chose which one you want to display and go back and forth between them.

SlideShare Presentations

SlideShare Presentations provides a way to not only upload and share PowerPoint presentations as with Google presentations, but you can additionally upload Word documents, PDFs, Keynote, and iWork pages, so you can upload portfolios, resume, conference talks, and marketing/sales presentations. You can even embed YouTube videos in presentations and add audio to make a webinar. And if you have a Facebook account, you can link the two, so once you upload a file to LinkedIn, Facebook, or SlideShare, it will appear on all three at once.

To add it, go to the Applications Directory and click on the logo or header.

Then, you'll see an explanation of SlideShare's features, including the supported file formats.

Once you add the application, you will be asked to enter your user name, email (it's best to use the email for your LinkedIn account).

Once you sign up, you can start uploading content, including multiple files at the same time.

Before you do upload content, however, it's a good idea to go to the SlideShare home page to synch SlideShare with your LinkedIn account. Once you synchronize them, your SlideShare presentations on LinkedIn will show up on SlideShare at www.slideshare.net on whatever user name you have created for the account.

The SlideShare Home Page also shows you the editor' favorite presentations under Editor's Picks for Today. These are the presentations uploaded by others in your industry and the latest presentations uploaded by your own LinkedIn connections.

To see previously uploaded presentations, go to Explore, which will first show you the most viewed.

You can see Slidecasts, which are slides linked to audios. These can be webinars, conference talks, musical slide shows, and other types of presentations. You have to create these presentations in SlideShare and then can add them to your LinkedIn profile, if you have synced your SlideShare account with your profile. You can also see slides with YouTube videos and create your own, though again, you have to have a Slideshare account synched with LinkedIn.

You can also see the Editors Picks for the last 6 months and the most downloaded presentations.

If you click on "Your Connections," you'll see the presentations your connections uploaded.

When you are ready to upload your own presentations, click the upload button. Then, you can browse and select files. Use the Ctrl key to upload multiple files at the same time.

After you have uploaded a file or files, enter a description about them, such as in the example, where I uploaded a .doc file with brief descriptions of books (AllSynopsis.doc) and a .PDF file with a sample from another book (17 Top Secrets-sample.pdf). After you fill in your description, indicate if you will permit others to download your file or not, and then click "publish" to complete the publishing process.

Once you hit "Publish" you will be advised that your slideshow is being converted and will be published shortly.

If you click "here," you will see the current status. Once it's completed, your uploaded file will appear on Your SlideSpace.

If you go to Your Application Settings, you can choose among various options, including whether you want to show the complete presentation or just the thumbnails, which is the default.

If you click on the thumbnail, you will see the complete presentation, as in the example below. Then, those who see it can recommend it, share it, or download it (if you have given them permission to do so). You can also bookmark it, tweet it, email it to your contacts, or add this to your profile, as in the example below for my book on "How to Keep Your Job or Find New Work."

If you add it to your profile, it will show up with a photo and title, which viewers can click to learn more. You can add up to three presentations to your profile.

By default, your presentation will show up as a thumbnail that people have to click to view. But if you make it available for view in the player, it will begin with a large image and a view of the cover sheet.

To delete a presentation, simply hit delete next to that presentation and it's gone.

Events

Events is a way to find events to go to or put on your own events.

To add an event, click on "Add an Event" and put in details about the event. Then you can promote this event to your network to up your attendance. Other people can comment on your event, and you can use these comments to add more buzz and excitement to the event. Another big advantage of being an event organizer is it features a link to your profile, along with your title, which helps to further promote you.

If you click on "Manage," you can update the event or edit information about it. To let your contacts know about the event, go to "Share" and invite them to spread the word.

You can also see the events that other people in your network are putting on, and you can let people know about events that you are going to. Or even if you are not going to an event, you can tell others about it if you think it's an interesting event, which can help you add value so people will want to look on you as a source of information.

Use the "Search" tab to find current and past events.

To sign up for Events, go to Applications Directory and click on the "Events" logo or headline.

You will then get this screen telling you about how the Events application works.

Once you sign-up, on the Events Home page, you'll see the events that the members of your network are putting on in the order in which they are occurring.

You will see the name and photo of the person posting the event and whether they are just interested the event, attending it, or organizing it. If you click on the person's name, that will take you to their profile.

You can see how many people are attending the event and learn more about the event, if you click on the title of the event.

If you click on the RSVP tab, you can see who has already RSVPed and the number in each of the categories -- attending, presenting, exhibiting, interested, not attending, and organizing the event.

You can then RSVP to indicate if you will be attending, presenting, exhibiting, or are just interested. To RSVP, click on the Overview tab or go back to the Event Home and RSVP there.

Once you RSVP, your name will appear on the list of different types of respondents on the Events Home page and in the complete RSVP list, which you can see if you click "See All RSPVs".

If you want to change your RSVP, say from being "interested" to "attending," or "attending" to not attending, you can easily do so, such as in my changing my RSVP from "attending" to "interested."

For example, you just have to click your current plans (ie: interested, attending) and your RSVP will change to that.

Or if you click "Undo" to cancel your reservation, it's gone.

You can find event within a certain period of time, location, and on a specific subject, if you go to "Find Events," whether you have a connection to anyone posting the event in your LinkedIn network or not. The default is all events occurring at any time anywhere.

You can specify when these events you are looking for might occur -- such as within a week, month, or year, and you can look for past events, too. You can specify a particular location, whether your own area or any other area. Also, indicate if you are interested in conferences, tradeshows and conventions, networking and Meetups, training and seminars, fundraisers, or other types of events.

Once you decide to participate in an event in any way -- from just being interested to attending or organizing it to not attending -- it'll show up on your My Events page, along with other information on the event, so anyone seeing the events you are attending can learn more and decide if they want to attend.

If you want to list an event, whether you're organizing it, attending, or simply interested, just go to the "Add an Event" tab. Then, enter the requested information about the event, including the title, date, time, venue, location, Website, and how you are participating in. Plus you can add other details about the event.

Once you have completed describing the event, you can directly publish it or preview it first.

If you preview the event, you can confirm and publish it, go back to edit it, or save the draft. The description only shows the first 300 characters, but people can click "Show More" to read the rest.

Once you publish the event, you'll see this screen, letting you know your event has been published. The announcement about it will go to everyone in your network. In addition, you can share the event with your contacts or advertise it through DirectAds on LinkedIn.

To share the event with your contacts, type in a name of specific contacts in your network. LinkedIn puts in a basic message you can send, though you can change and personalize it. You can add in a name of anyone in your network if you start to type a name.

Or click the "in" button to open up your list of contacts.

Your event will also show up on your My Events page, along with any other event which you have indicated you are participating in.

If you click on the event's title, you will see a full description of the listing, so others can RSVP if they wish. You will also be listed as attending the event.

To indicate that you are the event organizer, you can click "Claim this Event."

Once you do, you will be listed as the event organizer and invited to spread the word to your contacts, as noted above, or advertise on LinkedIn.

To share this event with contacts or advertise it, go back to the Manage tab for the event. If you decide to advertise it, you'll be invited to write your ad.

When you click "Next," you can opt to send your add to all LinkedIn members or target your audience.

If you advertise, you can set your ad budget, much as in Google AdWords, based on a minimum of $10.00 a day, plus a $50 minimum per ad.

As an example, suppose I want to set my budget at the $10 per day minimum, with a minimum of $3 per 1000 clicks. I'll be invited to put in my billing information with a minimum of $50 for 5 days. Thereafter I can end my ad at any time.

While your direct contacts will get the announcement of the event automatically, you can advertise the event to go to a larger targeted audience on LinkedIn.

You can also find out who in your network are interested in or will be attending events if you go to Browse Events, and scroll down to the Network Updates section.

You can find the events that are most popular for people in your network in a category, which you are interested in, such as Publishing in this example. Just click on the "Most Popular" tab, and you'll see events listed by the number attending.

Finally, you can use the "Find an Event" Search Box on your Events home page to find current and past events. This is a great way to get further details about an event if you have heard something about it but aren't sure where it is, the time, or who else in your network might be attending. Say you're interested in attending a dog show. Put "dog shows" into the Search Box to start searching.

You'll then get a list of events matching the type of event you are searching for:

If you know the name of a particular event, you can search by that.

You can narrow your search if you click on "Advanced Search." Then, you not only put in identifying information about the event you are looking for in Keywords, but you can indicate when the event is occurring (within a week to a year) or has occurred, where it is, and the type of event it is.

My Travel

My Travel by Tripit is a way to see where people in your network are traveling. This way, besides knowing where people are going, you can know when you'll be in the same city as your colleague, and if you have connections in other cities, you can let them know if you will be in that city and when.

To sign up, go the Applications Directory and click the "Tripit" icon or "My Travel" header.

You'll then see a brief description of how this application works by enabling you to list your upcoming trips and see who is close to where you are going.

Once you add the application, you'll see a screen inviting you to sign up, and if you have an upcoming trip planned, you can add that.

Once you sign up, TripIt will welcome you, and if you have listed an upcoming trip, TripIt will show all the people in your network, so you can invite them to use My Travel to set up meetings and networking opportunities. You can invite up to 50 people at a time, just as you can in sending direct emails to others in your network.

After you sign up to use this app, go to your email account to activate the application. Once it's activated, you'll get a notice about who is close to you. If you are connected to a large number of people in the area, you can click See All Matches to see a more extensive listing there. Then, if you click on the name of each person listed that will take you to their full profile.

You can also see the trips of others in your network who have signed up for My Travel.

If you click on that person's name, it will take you to their profile and will show you the trips they have been on or which are upcoming.

Your My Travel account will show up on your Home page and Profile, if you have checked this option, as in the example from my Home page where My Travel is featured under Polls. Besides seeing who is close to you, you can see how many people on your network are using My Travel -- in my case only 4%, and on your Full Profile, you can see how many miles you have traveled on trips you have already taken.

Box.net Files

Box.net Files is a way to manage your files online, including collaborating on them with friends and colleagues. To add the application, go to the Applications Directory and click on the "Box.net Files" logo or headline.

You'll get a short introduction on how Box.net works. Essentially, it lets you manage and share content online by storing your files online. Then, you can connect with others to collaborate, share, and access each others' important files securely and easily, from anywhere and for free. You can upload and manage your files through LinkedIn, so you can post files on your profile and share and collaborate with others on LinkedIn, as well as view and edit your files online.

Once you open up the application in LinkedIn, you'll see your LinkedIn profile in My Box. If you open the menu, it will show you various options.

Once you access your account on Box.net, you can upload files, create new folders, and add documents from the Web. Once you have created files and folders in the application, you can sort them by name, date, or size and add filters to show that these files are shared, used for collaboration, or starred. When you have multiple files, you can then tag them to more easily sort them later.

One way to organize the files you upload is to create a new folder for selected files. If you click New Folder, you can name the folder. To make it available for others to upload, download, share files, and edit within this fold, click "Editor" under Access Type. If you only want others to download and preview files in the folder, click "Viewer." To invite specific people, type in their emails.

You will then see a confirmation that you have added this folder and the number of people you have invited to share the folder with you.

You can invite other collaborators to share this with you if you click on "Shared", which will give you a secure link or this global to share it with everyone.

To make it global, click on "Customize this address and make global." Then create whatever name you want. Once you click okay, you are informed you now have a global folder.

After you invite the collaborators to join, they still have to do so. Until they do, you'll get a message that these users still need to join. Meanwhile, these invitees will get a message in their inbox -- and often their spam folder -- indicating that they have an invitation from you. If they open the email, they can simply click Accept Invitation to accept it and set up a BoxNet account, if they don't already have one. Note that the people you invite don't have to be on LinkedIn to become collaborators.

As people join, they will be added to your collaborators for that project, while anyone who hasn't yet joined will be indicated on the right side of your screen.

To upload files, click the "Upload" button and indicate what folder they are going in. If you upload them to All Files and Folders, they will only be viewable by you.

Box.net will then upload them and indicate once they are successfully uploaded.

After uploading, I can share any uploaded files with others, add a comment or tag to the file, edit, update, or delete. For example, if you click "Task", you can send a note to any or all collaborators telling them what to do, using a comment box or clicking on the Task Type Bar. You can select individual collaborators by typing the first letter of the name or email of each collaborator. Then check any collaborators you want to send the task to.

If there is more than one person, check in the box next to their name to add the selected person and their names will appear.

The task for the person to do with the file will appear in your projects folder, indicating who you sent the task to. There will be a "pending" sign next to that person's name until they respond to your request to perform the task.

Your request will appear like this in the collaborator's inbox.

Then, when your collaborator responds, he or she will get a request to do what you have asked (such as review the file), and then can either log in if he or she already has a Box.net account to review the file online or can create a new Box.net account by putting in a name and password.

Once the collaborator has signed in, he or she can respond to the task, and afterwards will see the response with an option to further edit this.

To share this file, click "Share." Then you can enter the emails for those you want to view the file and send a message.

Should you want to password protect the file, you have to upgrade to a paid account.

You can also embed the folder and its contents on your Website. Just click "Embed folder in your site" from the "All files and folders" section on LinkedIn.

To add more files to this folder or invite more collaborators, go back to that folder. You can create other tasks or share the folder or individual files with selected collaborators. You can highlight all of the files to perform the same operations with them at the same time, such as sending all of the files to collaborators to review or comment on.

If you go to "All files and folders," you can open a menu that will give you various options.

You will see the files you have added on LinkedIn, if you have linked Box.net to your LinkedIn account.

These folders will show up on your LinkedIn Home page, if you have checked this option, and those who click the folder, will see all the files you have included, as well as your collaborators.

You can select a file in Box.net to appear on your Profile page. Just select the folder you want displayed there. If another folder is already there, to change it click "select a folder". Then, click "Change" and select a New or Existing folder.

Then select the one you want to display.

That will change the display to the one you want, in this case the New Projects file.

You will then see the file in that folder on your LinkedIn Profile.

Later, as you add more folders and files, you can change what folder and files you display.

Reading List

Reading List by Amazon is another great tool, because it allows you to share the books you are reading or want to read on your profile.

This can help with your credibility and with connecting with others, because they can see what you are interested in and that you are reading good books. Some people will value knowing this, because they want to do business with someone who is professional and shares similar interests.

Listing your recommended or favorite books can also demonstrate that you know what you are talking about. For example, if someone in the IT field has listed several IT books they have read on their LinkedIn profile, this will impress others that they know their subject.

To sign into Reading List, just go to the More menu and the Applications Directory. Then click on the Reading List by Amazon Icon.

You will get a description of the app and an invitation to join. Just click to do so. Once you sign up for this application, as I have done, the invitation to join indicates you have done so and can go immediately to that application.

Once you sign up for the Reading List, it will appear on your More menu. Click to open it up, and you can start adding books. You will also see if there are news items or updates from your connections about the lists you are watching.

Say you decide to add *Outliers* by Malcolm Gladwell to your reading list. Put in the name of the book and click Search Books. You can then select from several choices, starting with the book you selected. Then Amazon suggests other books you might like -- in this case 289 pages! To see additional pages, click the arrow to the right. As you go along, you can select any books to add to your reading list or buy.

Once you select a book, you can indicate if you want to read it, are reading it, or have already read it. Plus, if you are reading the book on AMAZON's Kindle, you can indicate this, too.

If you want to learn about the Kindle or get one, AMAZON makes that easy for you -- just click Learn More for more information.

You can add your comments about any book you are recommending -- such as why you want to read it or why you think it is a great book.

Once you click "Save," the book is added to your reading list along with a photo of the book and your comment. Now you can add another book to your list.

If you click on "Your Reading List" tab, it'll show all the books, along with the number of books you have read and recommended.

Once you have read a book, you can opt to recommend it. Once you do, you will see the little thumbs up symbol, and your reading list will add this to the books you recommend.

Others who want to see your reading list will see a link from your home page, and they can click on "Your Reading List" to see what you are reading. If you want to delete a book from your list, just hit delete.

Polls

Polls are useful for getting some quick feedback on a product, service, or idea, since it allows you to conduct a poll in your network or with targeted professionals to get some market research data, as well as see the research results others have collected. However, you are limited to one question, so if you want more answers, you need to have a separate poll for each question or post a poll online and refer people in your network to that Website.

To sign up for this app, go to Polls in the Application Directory, click on the logo or headline.

You will then get an explanation of how Polls works. As the Polls description explains, you can for no charge, conduct a poll with your direct connections on LinkedIn , or you can conduct a poll with selected professionals that you define by industry, job title, company size, job function, age, gender, or geography, where you will pay per response, with at least a $50 minimum.

Once you add the Polls application, you can create a poll by asking a multiple choice question with up to five answers. You invite people to choose one of the five answers, and you can rotate the order of the answers, to avoid a bias whereby people might be more likely to say "yes" to the first answer. But you are limited to only one question with 5 alternatives for people to answer.

If you want to direct your poll to a target audience, you can send it to targeted LinkedIn members selected by company size, job function, industry, seniority, gender, age, and geography. The more specific your sample, the more you pay for each person who responds to the poll, ranging from a minimum of $1 a response to $5 a response if you use each category to narrow your sample. Or if you have a premium account, costing $25 to $500 a month, there's no charge.

To poll the people in your network at no charge, just indicate that you want to poll your first degree connections, and you can include the poll in your directory, so everyone on LinkedIn can view the poll and respond. When you have had enough results, you can end the poll.

Once you post a poll, you will be advised that the poll has been distributed to your network, and to further share the poll, you can include it on your blog or in an email.

You can see the poll on your profile and track the results on your home page and profile. Just scroll down to see where it is, which will depend on what other apps are on your home page or profile.

To see the number of responses, go to "Manage My Polls." If you have responded to a poll, you'll see that too.

If someone clicks on the poll, they will have an option to vote, such as below.

Once someone votes, it'll show up like this -- and you can even vote in your own poll.

But you can't vote more than once. If you do, such as when I tried to cast a vote for Facebook, I got this response, indicating that my most recent vote was not counted, because each person can only cast one vote. And you can't vote again on another computer, since your vote is tracked by your LinkedIn account.

You can also comment on and share the results of a poll.

To let people know about your poll, you can send everyone in your network an invitation, and you can add to the message below which LinkedIn fill in. You can also invite others not yet in your network to join in to participate in your poll.

The number of people who respond to your poll will depend on the size of your network and how interested they are in your poll. In my case, by the next day I had 8 responses, and the results looked like this. As might be expected, since I asked people on LinkedIn which social media they preferred, the vast majority -- 62% -- preferred LinkedIn, followed by Twitter or other social media.

These results include some demographics about the people responding to your poll -- their job type, company size, gender and age, which comes from the profile of each person voting. And people don't have to be part of your network to vote. They just have to be LinkedIn members, so they can view your full profile to vote. People can add comments when they vote, too.

To see the characteristics of the people participating in your sample, click on each of the categories -- for job type, company size, gender, and age.

You can also see other people's polls that were recently asked, vote on them, and see the results for information you can use yourself.

After I voted in the first poll, on which social network works best for your business, I found reinforcement for my own results -- with 83% of 8 respondents favoring LinkedIn.

In another poll, where the author wanted to learn how people used Facebook, I found that the vast majority of people -- 80% of 5 respondents, used it only for friends and family. Such information can be good to know if you are considering whether to put time and effort into using Facebook for business purposes, although you have to take into consideration that this is a poll of LinkedIn members, and they may not be interested in using another social media for their business since they already use LinkedIn.

If you scroll down in the "Browse Polls" section, you'll find other polls posted by people in your network.

Should someone make a comment, it will appear alongside their picture and job title.

While these polls appear to get only a handful of responses in a few days, if your poll is up for much longer, you will get a larger response. For example, the poll on considering the environment or sustainability drew 48 responses after it was posted for about seven months.

Besides asking general questions, you can ask what people think about your own product and service or about how it compares to a competitor's, as did an entrepreneur I know who sells an organizational system for performers did. She asked whether performers used her own system or that of a competitor, with these results.

In short, Polls can be a useful way to get a quick response from a small number of respondents about a single question, while seeing what others are interested in knowing about and the results. So if you've got a new product or service you want opinions about, this is a good way to get some market research data. And if you have more than one questions, ask each in a separate poll or direct respondents to a Website where you have a more complete poll posted online.

Part 4: Deciding On Your Strategy

Chapter 10: Deciding on the Best Strategy

The previous chapters have focused on the different tools and techniques you might use in a social media campaign through LinkedIn. This chapter focuses on how to choose what strategy to apply to your campaign.

LinkedIn's Tools and Techniques

Consider these different tools and techniques like having a toolbox or repertoire you can select from as needed. Then, consider how you might use them most effectively. Here are the major tools in your arsenal.

- creating a powerful LinkedIn profile (Chapter 1)
- creating a company profile (Chapter 2)
- getting and giving recommendations (Chapter 3)
- joining groups in your industry or your market (Chapter 4)
- connecting with members of groups (Chapter 5)
- inviting people you know to connect on LinkedIn (Chapter 5)
- starting your own group (Chapter 6)
- searching for contacts, work, companies, groups, and information (Chapter 7)

- asking questions and getting answers (Chapter 8)

- using applications for various purposes (Chapter 9)

  - Company Buzz to learn what people are saying about you

  - WordPress to create a blog

  - BlogLink to promote your blog on LinkedIn

  - Google Presentations to feature a PowerPoint presentation

  - SlideShare Presentations to share various types of presentations and files

  - Events to promote your events and learn what others are doing

  - My Travel to let people know where you are going, find out where others are going, and connect on your travels or theirs

  - Box.net files to share and collaborate on files online

  - Reading List to let others know what you are reading and recommend books

  - Polls to get feedback on your products, services, or ideas

Using LinkedIn with Other Social and Traditional Media

Consider LinkedIn an important part of your PR strategy, and sometimes the main or only promotional strategy. But more commonly, you might use LinkedIn along with other social media and traditional media to create a comprehensive PR campaign. By doing so, you reach people through multiple avenues, which can multiply the number of people who respond. Just as people may need to get several messages before they buy or do something -- commonly seven times for someone hearing or seeing a message to act -- so they may need to be contacted multiple times in multiple ways through LinkedIn, other social media, and sometimes the traditional media.

For example, say you hear about an upcoming conference in your area. While some people may immediately decide to go, others will just notice there is an upcoming conference; but without hearing more about it, they won't go. However, if they then get an email, see an article, and hear about it from people in their LinkedIn group, that will motivate them to go.

Accordingly, you can use multiple tools on LinkedIn to promote your company, product, or service, in addition to using other social media, such as Facebook or Twitter, or reaching out to the radio, TV, newspaper, magazine, and Internet media.

Getting Started

A first step is creating your personal profile and company profile, as discussed in Chapters 1 and 2. Create your profile as completely as possible, so when you direct people back to your profile, they will learn about what you do and the products or services you offer. Emphasize what is most relevant to the type of promotion you want, since in today's market of short attention spans, you want people to quickly get the main points. Also, highlight your recommendations, testimonials, honors, and awards, since these will help people in judging you and feeling assured in doing business with you. Not only your experience, but people's satisfaction with and praise for you will help them feel secure in the value you bring to working with them.

Every few weeks, keep your profile updated with new projects, new recommendations and testimonials, and new press materials, since this shows you are continually active and working on new projects or with new clients -- so people feel you are in demand. Paradoxically, the less it appears you need them for your success, the more others will feel they need you for theirs. Additionally, they will feel you are more special, and they will value what you do more. By making yourself seem more valued by others, you will be more valued by them.

Building Your Contacts and Group Connections

As you build and expand your profile, continually work on building your contacts and connections in groups you join or start yourself. And continually add to these online connections with the people you meet personally or in groups you join. As you can, reinforce your online connections with real-time meetings.

A key value of building your connections is you have more and more people to whom you can promote your products, services, events, and news about your company or yourself. Then, if people feel you are offering something valuable, they can promote it to their own contacts. So you spread the word virally.

But remember you have to nurture these relationships by contributing to a dialogue and adding value, so people build trust in you; don't just treat these connections as an advertising billboard, because you can turn everyone off, and they may come to think of you as a spammer. That's why it helps to mention useful information and news that might interest group members to build trust, rather than initially or only promoting yourself. If you take the time to build a relationship based on your providing value and creating trust, when you do promote yourself, people will be more receptive to what you have to say. So post regularly -- and if you can't always do it yourself, enlist an assistant to help you stay on the top of everyone's awareness.

As your connections and participation in groups grows, this is an ideal way to spread the news about your new products, services, events, books, or whatever else you are doing. You can post announcements or create and promote events. Creating a group can bring together people who are especially interested in what you are doing, and your group is an ideal vehicle for promoting your events or other business activities.

Using Search, Questions, and Other Applications

Search can help you further build your network through finding people to connect to and groups in your field you can join. Depending on your business, you can target your search locally, nationally, or even internationally.

Besides asking questions for information, you can answer questions yourself or recommend others to show off your expertise, which can help people further trust and value you. However, don't only use answers to directly promote your product or service -- such as advising people to buy your product, use your service, or look to your book for what they need. Instead, give valuable information to help answer a person's questions. Then, they are apt to be receptive when you indicate how you can give them further help.

Finally, you can use many of the applications on LinkedIn to help your promotion in various ways.

- Use CompanyBuzz to hear what people are saying about you; WordPress to create a blog with information related to whatever you are promoting; and Blog Link to feature your blog if it's not on WordPress.
- Use Google Presentation and SlideShare Presentations to feature PowerPoints, Videos, Photos, and other materials that show what you are doing.
- Use Events to find out about events you might want to attend, learn what events your connections are attending so you might join them or discuss these events with them, or create and promote your own events.
- Use My Travel to make connections in cities where you are going by letting your network connections know where you will be and when, so they can connect with you.
- Use Box.net Files to share documents with others.
- Use Reading List to let others know what you are reading and would recommend to others to create a closer bond with them.

- Use Polls to learn what others are saying about questions you have or get some quick feedback about your own ideas.

Using Your Home Page to Build Your Connections

LinkedIn can help you continue to build your connection if you keep up with the changes on your home page. Here are some of things you can do on a regular basis.

Check Your Inbox

Messages to you will turn up in your email box or you can track them online. Then, take appropriate action to respond or archive the message. A good way to build your network is to invite anyone who sends you a message to invite you to connect. If they do, accept and that's one more connection in your network.

Send an Invitation to Connect to the "People You May Know"

You'll find different people suggested each time you open or go to your home page. They will be listed by their level of connection to you -- 2nd, 3rd, or group, and you can mention that in your invite. Click "See more" for even more people to invite.

Check your Network Updates and Add to Them.

Often you will find information about what you are doing automatically updated if you have connected your LinkedIn account to other social media, such as Twitter. For instance, I'm connected to Twitter and have been submitting articles to EzineArticles which has a feed to Twitter. So whenever I post a new article that is accepted on Ezines, it appears on LinkedIn, such as when I wrote "The Appeal of Investing in Films." You can also add your own updates by posting them directly on LinkedIn or using Ping to post each update on all your social media accounts.

You simply enter your updated information in the Network Updates box, limiting your post to 140 characters, click share, and there it is.

Check the Status, Profile, Group, Connection, and Event Updates

Here's how to deal with each of these types of updates.

For **Status Updates**, which let you know what your connections are doing, you can click on the person's name to go to their profile. If you click on Reply Privately, you can send that person a message, or to include others, click: "Include others in this message" to add them.

If you want, add a comment, which will go on your LinkedIn profile, and the other person will see it, too.

In the case of **Profile Updates**, you will see when people change their profiles or have an updated title. You can send them a message to congratulate them and can personalize your message, too.

In the case of **Group Updates**, you can see the latest groups your direct connections have joined.

If you click on the name of those groups where you aren't already a member, you can ask to join that group, such as in the example below where I have clicked on "Media Leaders."

In the case of **Event Updates,** you will see the latest news about the events your direct connections are participating in as attendees, exhibitors, or organizers. Then, if you are interested, you can follow up and let your connections know or click on the event to contact the organizers directly. If you want to attend, you can RSVP yourself. For instance, when I saw that a friend was attending the Los Angeles

Women's International Spring Gala Event, I clicked on the event to learn more.

In the case of **Connection Updates**, you will see who the people in your network have recently connected to, so you can invite them if desired to connect directly to you -- another good way to further build your network. Just click on that person's name to see their profile (View Profile) or send them an invitation to connect (Invite to Connect).

Group Updates for Your Group Activities

Besides the previous Group Updates section featuring what your connections are doing, if you go to the Group Updates section which lists the groups you belong to, you can see the latest discussions initiated by the members of your groups -- the same discussion updates that are sent to your email if you have checked this option. You can click on the title of the discussion to follow that discussion or add your own comment.

Check on Views of Your Profile

You can check on "Who's Viewed My Profile" to learn who has looked at your profile or how often you have appeared in search results, so you can contact them to follow up if you wish. Click "See more" to get some general information about the companies of the people who have viewed your profile. While they could contact you if they wanted to do so, if you want to follow up directly, you have to upgrade your account to see more.

Check for Updates on Your Applications

You'll see the highlights for the applications listed on your home page, such as **Events, Answers** and your **WordPress** files. Click on that application to learn more.

In short, LinkedIn can provide you with a variety of tools and techniques to use in a variety of ways to promote your business or yourself, though the way you use them depends very much on what you want to promote and what else you are doing for your promotion. Whatever you do, LinkedIn can be a great supplement to use in conjunction with other social media, such as Facebook, Twitter, and Plaxo, and with the traditional media, including newspapers, magazines, radio, TV, and the Internet. Just think of LinkedIn as having an arsenal of promotional weapons or a repertoire of methods you can draw on. The particular ones you choose are up to you, depending on what you want to promote and how.

Chapter 11: Assessing Your Campaign

From time to time, see how your LinkedIn campaign is going. Key indicators to look at are:

The Size of Your Network

How is your campaign to build your network going? Look at both the size of your direct or 1st level connections and at the size of your expanded network of 2nd and 3rd level connections. As your network grows, you will soon go from a few hundred on your 1st level to thousands on your 2nd level to even millions on your 3rd level. When you figure in your group connections, you could potentially be able to reach multimillions.

To check your stats, go to your "Contacts" tab, and then to "Network Statistics."

When you click on Network Statistics, you'll see how well you are doing.

The Number and Type of Responses

Besides the size of your network, look at the number and type of responses you are getting from your LinkedIn campaign. Consider if you are getting good leads to opportunities, events, prospective customers, and clients; if so, that's a good sign to keep going with your current campaign. If not, consider what you might do to make your campaign more effective, such as changing your message or your offerings to your targeted audience.

Also, look at how successfully your connections are leading to customers and clients, and consider the costs of acquiring them, including the time you are investing into the campaign. For example, notice how many leads you are getting from your direct and other connections and how many prospective customers or clients are contacting you as a result of being connected to you or finding your profile on LinkedIn. Additionally, keep track of how many leads are turning into actual customers or clients, how much they are paying for services or products, and how their purchases compare to those of customers or clients obtained from other sources.

Increasing Awareness and Brand Identity

If your campaign is more about awareness, brand identity, and establishing a presence, notice how well that is going. Are people are more aware of your business or of you as a result of your LinkedIn presence? Is there an increase in people contacting you as an expert, speaker, presenter, panelist, or interviewee for the print media or for a radio or TV program?

A campaign could be very effective in building up your company or you as a leader or expert in your field, though it isn't resulting in immediately getting more customers or clients and increasing sales. But then that increased awareness could turn into increased perceived value, leading to more sales or increased pricing for your products or services.

Using Your Analysis to Decide What to Do

Doing this analysis of your PR campaign will help you to assess how well it is working by examining whether it is resulting in more clients and customers, more sales, or a greater presence and perceived value for whatever you do.

Then, based on the results and your goals and expectations, you can decide what to do to make your PR campaign more effective, whatever combination of social and traditional media you are using or plan to use in the future.

Other Books By The Author

Here are other books on achieving success or improving work relationships by the author:

- *DOING YOUR OWN PR*
- *WANT IT, SEE IT, GET IT! VISUALIZE YOUR WAY TO SUCCESS*
- *ENJOY: 101 LITTLE THINGS TO ADD FUN TO YOUR WORK EVERYDAY*
- *30 DAYS TO A MORE POWERFUL MEMORY*
- *DISAGREEMENTS, DISPUTES, AND ALL-OUT WAR*
- *A SURVIVAL GUIDE FOR WORKING WITH HUMANS*
- *A SURVIVAL GUIDE FOR WORKING WITH BAD BOSSES*
- *A SURVIVAL GUIDE TO MANAGING EMPLOYEES FROM HELL*
- *17 TOP SECRETS FOR HOW TO KEEP YOUR JOB OR FIND NEW WORK TODAY*
- *LET'S HAVE A SALES PARTY*
- *SUCCESS IN MLM, NETWORK MARKETING, AND PERSONAL SELLING*

Author Contact Information

Here's how to contact the author for information about other books and about speaking for your organization or putting on workshops and seminars for your organization:

> Gini Graham Scott, Ph.D.
> Director
> Changemakers
> 6114 La Salle, #358
> Oakland, CA 94611
> (510) 339-1625, FAX: (510) 339-1626
> changemakers@pacbell.net
> www.ginigrahamscott.com

Or visit Gini Graham Scott's Websites for her books:

www.workwithgini.com (books on improving work relationships)

www.wantitseeitgetit.com (featuring *Want It, See It, Get It!*)

www.enjoythebook.com (featuring *Enjoy! 101 Little Ways to Add Fun to Your Work Everyday*)

www.badbosses.net (featuring *A Survival Guide for Working with Bad Bosses*) www.workingwithhumans.com (featuring *A Survival Guide for Working with Humans, A Survival Guide to Managing Employees from Hell,* and *Disagreements, Disputes, and All Out War)*

www.topsecretsbooks.com (featuring books on sales, marketing, and PR)

Lightning Source UK Ltd.
Milton Keynes UK
16 November 2010

162943UK00007B/88/P